ARTS AND CRAFTS MASTER

The Houses and Gardens of

M. H. BAILLIE SCOTT

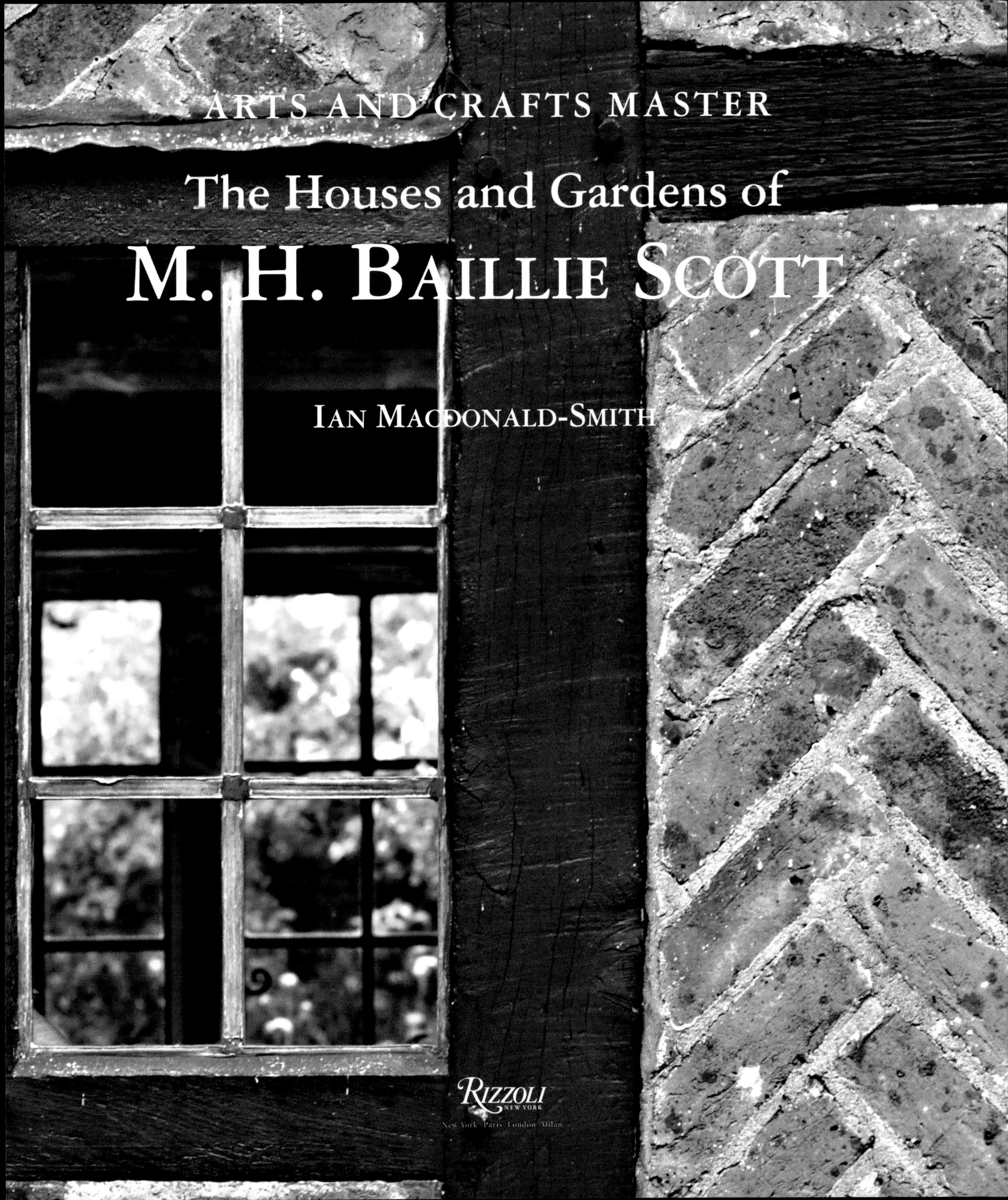

ARTS AND CRAFTS MASTER

The Houses and Gardens of

M. H. BAILLIE SCOTT

IAN MACDONALD-SMITH

RIZZOLI
NEW YORK

New York · Paris · London · Milan

First published in the United States of America in 2010 by
Rizzoli International Publications, Inc.
300 Park Avenue South
New York, NY 10010
www.rizzoliusa.com

ISBN: 978-0-8478-3181-4
LCCN: 2009942073

Distributed to the U.S. trade by
Random House, New York

Printed and bound in China

2010 2011 2012 2013 2014 / 10 9 8 7 6 5 4 3 2 1

PAGE 1 *Left: One of six finely carved repeating
patterns in the living room paneling wainscot at Ivydene.
Right: Detail of carving on the hallway fireplace with a
lovingly rubbed nose at Ivydene.*

PAGES 2–3 *Detail of a window at Great Wood. Typical of
Baillie Scott are houses that are one room wide, allowing
light to enter from two facades.*

RIGHT *Detail of the exquisite inlay in a Baillie Scott–
designed cabinet at Waldbühl that has an anthropomorphic
quality transcending the mere representation of leaves and
flowers.*

Contents

Introduction

The term Arts and Crafts was first coined in 1888 by the Arts and Crafts Exhibition Society, which consisted of a group of dissidents who were indignant at the Royal Academy's refusal to exhibit the work of William Morris, Philip Webb, Ernest Gimson, and C. R. Ashbee, among others. Since 1882, various guilds were formed, and two of the five most significant were founded by architects. One of these two was founded by A. H. Mackmurdo, whose self-described mandate was to "render all branches of art the sphere no longer of the tradesman but of the artist. It would restore building, decoration, glass painting, pottery, woodcarving and metal to their place beside painting and sculpture." The opportunity was laid bare for young avant-garde architects to take advantage of this movement because it embraced the promotion of art and beauty in every aspect of design and lent itself admirably to the much-needed injection of fresh ideas in the stagnating pool of Victorian architecture.

At the turn of the twentieth century there were three prominent young architects of the Arts and Crafts movement: C. F. A. Voysey, Charles Rennie Mackintosh, and M. H. Baillie Scott. All three architects possessed unique and identifiable styles and are loosely classified as "Free Style," Voysey was known as a purveyor of the vernacular; Mackintosh as progressive, avant-garde, and a practitioner of Art Nouveau; and Baillie Scott fits comfortably between the two. Baillie Scott influenced many of the great architects of the late nineteenth and early twentieth centuries. While he is credited alongside Frank Lloyd Wright as being the innovator of open-plan interiors, Baillie Scott is acknowledged to be without peer in this regard and in fact initially influenced Wright.

The Arts and Crafts movement has been largely misunderstood in architectural history mainly due to the emphasis given to the resistance against mass production of decoration in the Victorian era rather than its major success in widely influencing modern architecture. The movement's negative reaction to mass production is still remarkably appropriate today from the perspective that it was concerned that cheap goods are indiscriminately produced that are passed off as art but which derive from original craftsmanship.

And here is where the misunderstanding lies: the movement was not looking backward to a time before the machine age but forward to a time when art would flourish and the practice of ancient building crafts would thrive. Baillie Scott, before Adolf Loos and Frank Lloyd Wright, was the most vocal advocate within the Arts and Crafts movement, cautioning in his book *Houses and Gardens* that excellence would not be created through "costliness of material and workmanship, or, failing that, an imitation of such costliness. We dream a dream of marble halls, and we realize as a practical result of such a dream a hall with marbled wallpaper—and a hatstand! . . . Let us rather set up as an ideal such a humble standard as is implied in the mere omission of the vulgar, and then when our homes are purged of all vulgar and painful things, let us add by slow degrees with careful and exclusive choosing, such few and choice ornaments as may be required."

Mackay Hugh Baillie Scott was born at Beards Hill, St. Peter's, near Ramsgate, Kent, England, on October 23, 1865, the first child of fourteen to a wealthy Scottish baron of the same name. He was groomed to manage the family sheep farm in Australia and in 1883 was sent to the Royal Agricultural College at Cirencester. He excelled and graduated with honors but came to realize that farming was not the future that he wanted for himself, luckily for the architectural world.

He went to Bath as an articled pupil to Major Charles Davis, the City Architect from 1886 until 1889. Davis was not well respected or liked by Baillie Scott, and history similarly has not been complimentary to the City Architect. It was in Bath that Baillie Scott met and courted Florence Nash, whom he married in 1889. They honeymooned on the Isle of Man. He maintained that he was so seasick that he could not bear the thought of the

return voyage to the mainland, thus explaining his stay on the island for the following twelve years. There he secured employment working for Fred Saunderson and by 1890 he was accepting his own commissions. Baillie Scott met Archibald Knox, the famous Liberty & Co. designer, while attending classes at Isle of Man School of Art in the island's capital, Douglas, and subsequently collaborated with Knox on design details for the architect's early commissions. Knox is acknowledged to be the first true influence on Baillie Scott.

Baillie Scott and his wife lived on the Isle of Man from 1889 until 1901. He always said that the reason for leaving was that too many local architects and builders were copying his style, but it is now thought that it was the collapse of a local bank that made the decision for him. He only designed twelve buildings and a smattering of interiors on the Isle of Man in those twelve years, indicating that the local population was less than supportive of his style. In the time he was on the Isle of Man most of his commissions were overseas, and these are the most innovative of his career. He also published many articles in *The Studio* magazine, which was widely circulated and resulted in significant international commissions. This was, however, a mixed blessing, as his designs were widely copied, which led him to cease submitting articles and drawings to the magazine. It could be said that Baillie Scott was the first truly international architect with almost three hundred commissions ranging from the Isle of Man to England, Scotland, Wales, Russia, Romania, Poland, Austria, Germany, France, Switzerland, Belgium, Italy, America, Canada, New Zealand, Hong Kong, and Peru!

His first commission on the mainland was Bexton Croft, which he managed to secure by forming a partnership with Henry Morris, an associate from Bath. Bexton Croft was a success, but the partnership ended in 1897, the year Baillie Scott received his first significant European commission from the Grand Duke Ernst Ludwig of Hesse, a grandson of Queen Victoria, to design the furniture and decorate the drawing room and dining room in the Grand Ducal Palace at Darmstadt. The following year he received another commission from the Grand Duke's sister, the Crown Princess Marie of Romania, to create Le Nid, a fantasy tree house. It was primarily due to these commissions that Baillie Scott first became a fashionable and highly sought-after architect in Europe.

Baillie Scott was also an innovator with his exterior designs, and the progressiveness of his exteriors can be seen at three significant houses: White Lodge, White House, and Danestream. The architect produced subtle but revolutionary concepts ahead of his peers such as sheathing the entire structure in harled roughcast, or pebbledash, using long steeply pitched roofs with minimal eave overhang, setting windows flush to the wall surface, and employing simple rectangular chimneys. Baillie Scott did this effectively, making truly modern, simple sculptural forms with crisp, sharp edges and angular planes, thus creating houses that were almost purely geometrical, foreshadowing the cubist movement in painting and certainly setting a direction for the puritanically stark buildings of the modernist movement.

One of Baillie Scott's overriding principles, set forth in *Houses and Gardens*, was that "there should be no arbitrary division between construction and decoration. . . . Everywhere construction is decorative and decoration constructive, and when the builder's work is done the paperhanger and painter only help, by pattern and colour, to put finishing touches to a construction which has already gone far to make the building beautiful."

In 1901 Baillie Scott entered an international competition created by the editor of *Zeitschrift für Innendekoration*, a magazine published in Darmstadt, to design a "Haus eines Kunstfreundes," or "House for an Art Lover." The aim of the competition was "to contribute energetically to the solution of important questions confronting modern architecture." No first prize was awarded as the judges deemed that none of the designs quite hit the mark, however, Baillie Scott received the highest prize awarded, with the judges praising his "masterfully handled interiors." Charles Rennie Mackintosh also entered the competition and was disqualified for not having the requisite interior plans but did receive a prize as well.

In 1898 Baillie Scott hired Wilfred Bond, whom he met on the Isle of Man, to supervise his commissions on mainland England. This worked effectively until Baillie Scott moved to Bedford in 1901. The logistics of managing commissions from the Isle of Man, the unabashed plagiarism of his designs, and the collapse of a local bank all contributed to the move to Bedford, but the primary motivation for the move was close proximity to the Pyghtle Works and the relationship that Baillie Scott had nurtured with the owner, J. P. White, for whom he had designed furniture since 1898. By 1901 a sales catalogue was published with 120 pieces of furniture designed solely by the architect, a significant accomplishment for Baillie Scott. Very few of the pieces are known to survive, and it is thought that some of his designs were too progressive for the turn-of-the-century marketplace.

It was at this time that Baillie Scott's success reached its pinnacle with international commissions, widely published work, furniture commissions, recognition from his peers, and the inevitable imitation by lesser designers. However, Baillie Scott's acceptance into Bedford life was less than spectacular. He never managed to procure a commission for a project there and only managed two commissions for small but exquisite cottages in nearby Biddenham. This was in part due to the stuffy conventions of Victorian England, whose middle classes preferred to let the Empire circumscribe their outlook with introspective rigidity and chauvinism rather than look outward toward a new way of living.

This may have been the turning point in Baillie Scott's career, at which he dressed his brilliant and innovative interior planning in old clothes. The architect had always had a penchant for old country houses, and when he returned to the mainland perhaps saw the opportunity to build houses in the local material and close to the vernacular but with his brilliant subtlety. He was a firm proponent of trusted materials: stone, brick, oak, and tile. He had looked at half-timbered construction that had survived well for hundreds of years and understood that if his houses were built with the same integrity they too would last for centuries. He also understood the intrinsic quality of great craftsmanship and how it permeates a space and the inhabitants.

Shortly after returning to England, Baillie Scott was invited to participate in the Garden City movement. In 1904 the architect designed several houses for Letchworth, located near Bedford, and two in Hampstead, London, in 1906. The architects Barry Parker and Raymond Unwin were the leading architects for the suburb, which was the brainchild of Ebenezer Howard. His revolutionary idea was to provide reasonably sized plots for houses of modest proportions, allowing them the fresh air and space that he thought necessary for a balanced life. Waterlow Court in the Hampstead Garden Suburb is Baillie Scott's most successful and complete rendition of low-cost housing. The design is revolutionary, with fifty small dwelling units surrounding a courtyard, which fosters a sense of open space and individual ownership as well as offering relief from the squalor of the terrace housing designed by builders little interested in the conditions of the occupants. Waterlow Court was designed for single working women, a rarity outside middle class dwellings where they were essentially indentured servants with few liberties. Baillie Scott created a community where there were individual plots for gardening, a dining refectory, and a common sitting room that allowed for more convenient and economical living that offered a degree of dignity that is taken for granted now. It was a successful social experiment that ushered in some less successful urban mass-housing schemes that failed to emulate Baillie Scott's highly refined work.

The main hall at Ockhams, where Baillie Scott lived for twenty-two years. The architect's personal 1933 copy of Houses and Gardens *rests on the gateleg table thought to have been used in many of the interior photographs of the book.*

*Detail of a stained-glass window in Dove's
Nest with motifs of hearts, birds, and tulips,
typical of Baillie Scott's designs.*

Baillie Scott was also an architectural historian and critic—in 1906 he published *Houses and Gardens*, in which he put forward his theories on all aspects of architecture and, more importantly, the application of good design and planning as a way of life. *Houses and Gardens* is still widely regarded as the best reference book for authentic Arts and Crafts theory. Baillie Scott's inclination toward innovation prepared him to embrace new technology and advocate the efficient use of space in small domestic situations. He saw no reason to spend money on furniture when a room could be designed with much of the necessary furniture built in. He practiced what he preached until the end of his career, with bay window seating and dining recesses and inglenooks creating cozy rooms within rooms. Contemporary architect and critic Hermann Muthesius wrote of Baillie Scott's rooms, "He never thinks in terms of unfurnished spaces; rather he always has the complete, furnished and inhabited room in mind when he designs."

He embraced double glazing and designs that took into consideration how animals entered and exited the house without human intervention—we now call them "cat flaps." His well-considered philosophies remain valid today for their emphasis on efficient use of space, honest materials that stand the test of time, and a true sense of what is important and practical for modest living. He berated builders for failing to consider the needs of their houses' occupants and provided formulas for design depending on where the entry was on a terraced house, something that had never been considered in 1906 and a concept that is little practiced today!

Houses and Gardens was well received in Europe and in the United States. The book was translated into German and it was in Germany where it had its most profound influence. After its publication Baillie Scott was followed by designers who would become the most influential figures in architecture during the twentieth century and was acknowledged either directly or subsequently through the designs that have unquestionable provenance. To have influenced Mackintosh, Wright, Voysey, Knox, Mies van der Rohe, Le Corbusier, Adolf Loos, Peter Behrens, J. J. P. Oud, and the architects of the Bauhaus and the International Style is remarkable.

In 1905 Baillie Scott's practice expanded when he hired Alfred Beresford to be his chief assistant. Beresford had extensive experience as a builder and carpenter, had studied extensively, and had worked on the restoration of some old Cheshire farmhouses, which suited the direction that Baillie Scott decided to pursue. It is ironic that after such an innovative and fresh start to his career the architect gravitated to an antiquated feel while still retaining his refined principles of interior planning. The architectural world will never know the reasons for the departure, but it was Beresford who allowed Baillie Scott to concentrate on his work as a designer; Beresford was much more practical and organized than Baillie Scott, who recognized these qualities. In 1919, after the Great War, when Baillie Scott resumed his practice he made Beresford a partner. Baillie Scott also hired more highly trained assistants, particularly Jack Pocock, who was responsible for teaching the craftsmen working on Baillie Scott's projects precisely how the demanding architect wanted his plans executed. The resulting high quality is evident today and still impresses experts.

In fact, thanks to catastrophic fortune, no one has a true grasp of Baillie Scott's genius. First in 1911 he suffered a fire at Fenlake Manor, his home and office. Then, to add insult to injury, the firm's office at Gray's Inn was bombed in 1939 during the Blitz of London, and Baillie Scott's archives were destroyed. He retired in 1939 after an extraordinary fifty-year career. Since then many of his houses have been modified, some beyond recognition. Many of his commissions cannot be found, and many in Germany were bombed during World War II.

During the Great War the Baillie Scotts moved continually, never settling for more than a few months. In 1920, however, the family found Oakhams, a fifteenth-century farmhouse near Edenbridge, Kent, where they settled until 1942. It was here that Baillie Scott was able to crystallize his thoughts about old buildings and grew to appreciate the beauty and integrity that these buildings possessed and which represented an unattainable standard. Baillie Scott certainly pursued this ideal with the same degree of vigor that he had previously devoted to innovation. It was an understanding that few could have synthesized so well, combining so many styles in a seemingly unified whole.

After the Great War, Baillie Scott established his practice at 8 Grays Inn, Holborn, and the practice thrived with 130 houses completed between 1919 and 1939, when the firm dissolved. It was after 1919 that Baillie Scott embarked on a campaign against building codes and bylaws. He saw these as too restrictive to allow any architect the freedom to express ideas without constraints from bureaucrats who had little sensitivity toward creativity and individual tastes and desires. This culminated in 1929 with a speech to the Royal Institute of British Architects and a related article titled "Are Building Bye-laws Destructive of Rural Beauty?"

Occasionally he found clients who could afford his passion for building with salvaged material. Longburton House in Dorset is a fine example, with almost all of the house built from recovered material. Baillie Scott's sensitivity to the vernacular rural aesthetic is considered a blemish in a remarkable career but, if anything, it demonstrates the architect's versatility and his sensitivity to the environment as well as the desire to remedy the senseless attrition of the Great War with a sense of order that was to be found in a simpler and quieter life. The great loss of life had changed the social landscape. No longer was it acceptable to maintain old class divisions, and many of Baillie Scott's clients in the postwar period were middle-class, affluent enough to afford the staff to maintain a lifestyle unfamiliar to most households today. (All of Baillie Scott's kitchens and bathrooms have been updated to reflect modern needs and the architect would have embraced the changes and designed accordingly.)

Baillie Scott's best designs were executed between 1892 and 1914, with the common academic wisdom dictating that his best work was done before 1907. After 1913 there was a demand for neo-Georgian houses, and Baillie Scott succumbed to the pressure to design in this idiom. It is not clear whether he executed the designs but it must be assumed that it was not, as these houses oppose his sensibilities. In 1933 Baillie Scott, with Beresford, published a revised edition of *Houses and Gardens*. It seems that this publication was an attempt to gain more commissions but it was not well received. While the initial publication was a treatise that was revolutionary and fresh, the revised edition was a weak defense of that position illustrated with houses and designs that did not demonstrate the integrity of those illustrating the first edition.

By 1935 Baillie Scott was little enamored with architecture and design and was rarely seen in the office, which had been relocated to Bedford Row in 1930. He spent more time painting and in 1939, after the death of his wife and the outbreak of World War II, Baillie Scott officially retired from the practice. At the end of his career Baillie Scott was out of touch with the fast pace of change in the architectural world. He was determined to advocate for a style that was no longer modern. It is perhaps this intransigence that caused Baillie Scott to fade into relative obscurity for so long.

What is beyond doubt is Baillie Scott's contribution to modern architecture as artist, architect, and architectural historian. It was fortuitous for Baillie Scott and the architectural world that he was in the right place at the right time with the right skills to influence so much. While the Arts and Crafts movement is one of the pivotal movements in architectural history, influencing so much of the twentieth century, it is ironic that Baillie Scott is perhaps the least-known and respected of the Arts and Crafts architects though he made the biggest contribution to the movement and its future influence, being overshadowed by Mackintosh, Wright, Voysey, and Edwin Lutyens, none of whom had Baillie Scott's skill and vision in interior planning.

Baillie Scott's influence on Mackintosh, Wright, the Bauhaus movement, the Darmstadt community, Loos, Behrens, Le Corbusier. and Mies makes him a truly extraordinary figure. The endeavor of this book is to provide further insight into Baillie Scott's work and his contribution to the development of twentieth-century architecture. The Arts and Crafts movement is unique in architectural history for its advocacy of adequate, comfortable, and well-planned housing for the average family with the intention of improving the whole of society. The movement did not succeed in its aims, but it set precedents, benchmarks, and standards that still are relevant. The movement railed against Victorian mass production of cheap products and against builders who produced poorly planned dwellings with the sole intention of maximizing profit.

Baillie Scott's use of local building materials and his understanding of the durability and structural qualities of flint, brick, stone, and oak are remarkable. In his adherence to the honesty of materials he surpasses Wright, many of whose houses are now suffering for the architect's choice of materials, and which few of Baillie Scott's houses suffer. Also worth noting is the degree to which Baillie Scott understood the value of craft and the skills of good craftsmen—he always wanted the very best, and as a result the current owners of these houses benefit from his demanding standards. After World War I, when fewer craftsmen were available, Baillie Scott still managed to find the skilled labor capable of executing his designs, though more than once his exacting standards almost bankrupted the builder. A hundred years on roofs may need retiling and windows releading, but the houses' structural integrity endures. Walking into a Baillie Scott house leaves no doubt who its architect is. The consistency of the detailing between the houses is intriguing. While the best houses may have been designed and built by 1907, many of the same details are found in his houses up to 1937.

Professor James Kornwolf in 1970 embarked on an odyssey to rediscover Baillie Scott. His book *M. H. Baillie Scott and the Arts and Crafts Movement* is the definitive work on the architect and admirably provides the discourse on Baillie Scott's important place in architectural history. Kornwolf's journey was remarkable and a true labor of love, and one that thirty-five years later I endeavored to undertake again. For this journey, however, I had the modern advantage of GPS navigation, and even then it was not easy to find many of these houses. How-

ever, there were many times when an instinct derived from Baillie Scott's philosophies seemed to guide me to these enchanting houses. They were inevitably situated in fine locations on a south-facing hill, close enough to civilization but far enough away to enjoy the illusion of isolation and peaceful existence with nature.

In addition to the aforementioned south-facing hills, the houses share proximity to towns, but at a polite distance, and many are exquisitely situated with stunning views. Almost all of the houses pay homage to their local architectural environment—Baillie Scott was skilled in both nestling each structure into its environment and complementing the local vernacular, taking cues without being slavish, and adding a hint of rebellion, a wink of humor, and all with a strong Arts and Crafts fingerprint.

As this book unfolds you will see many common features that in combination make the houses identifiable and unique. They are, in no particular order: heavy oak front doors, half-timbering, long sloping roofs, interconnecting living and dining rooms, heart-shaped motifs, strap hinges, a range of newel posts, decorative plaster, oak paneling, liberal use of quarter-sawn oak, ironwork, barrel-vaulted ceilings, great halls, generous U-landings on staircases that fiunction as small rooms, minstrels' galleries, leaded glass windows, inglenooks, stained glass, bay windows, window vents, carving, north-facing access hallways, south-facing principal rooms, proportionate windows (cooling in summer, warming in winter), garden rooms, loggias and sunrooms, well-considered garden planning, dormer windows, beamed ceilings, exposed interior structure, fitted and built-in cupboards, copper repoussé hoods, yew hedges, and in many cases the use of local building materials.

Experiencing the overlapping details in Baillie Scott's houses is wonderfully enlightening. While collecting the images for this book, it was a joy to find details in one house that existed in another. The project became a treasure hunt, and only after visiting most of the houses does one recognize unique details that lie outside of the Baillie Scott idiom, which in itself is so rich. It is in the details that Baillie Scott shines and allows the houses' inhabitants to enjoy living in a virtually constant state of discovery. Many of the owners of these houses have only a partial appreciation of the architect's true genius, with some living in their houses for years without realizing who designed their home.

James Kornwolf, Diane Haigh, and Greg Slater have all devoted a significant part of their academic and architectural credentials and experience to preserving Baillie Scott's legacy. I differ significantly in that my only qualification is to have

Whimsical carving on the newel post at King's Close.

lived in one of these incredible houses. My first memory of Havisham House, aged three or four, is walking up the stairs and being awed by the corridor, which disappeared into darkness, an indoor athletic track for toddlers. As children we were constantly being told not to use it as such, which seemed completely illogical.

Growing up in a Baillie Scott house was a privilege, and from the experience one gains a deep understanding of what makes quality construction. When my parents renovated Havisham House and wanted to insert two small windows in two of the primary bedrooms, it took the builders two days to jackhammer through the flint and mortar. The house is solid, well considered, well built to the extent that very little care and attention needs to be taken regarding the structure of the house.

I grew up with stories of how my grandfather always had seen the house designed by Baillie Scott called Michael's and one day with my grandmother and aunt knocked on the door of the disheveled house. The owner liked the family so much that she decided to sell Michael's. She had occupied only two rooms, and the remainder of the house was covered in cobwebs, so the first task was to explore the rest of the rambling struc-

ture. It was this exercise that inspired my grandmother to change the name to Havisham House, after Miss Havisham in *Great Expectations.*

I never tired of encountering this organism, seeing it differently every time I looked, and I have long wanted to find a way to express the sensation of inhabiting these beautiful and practical works of art. To be able to live in a structure of this quality, to be cocooned by it, protected by it, to love it enough to talk to it, is an extraordinary form of neurosis that I'm quite prepared to admit to! It is humbling to realize the great privilege of living in comfort within a structure that is appropriate and fulfills all of the necessary functions and that is built with the quality of material and construction to see it easily and well maintained. Such amenities need not belong exclusively to grand structures, and it is a way of living to which I believe all should have access.

Baillie Scott fundamentally understood the sustainable aspect of his house designs, and his theories have been validated by the sheer number of his houses that are still in remarkable condition. As poet John Betjeman wrote of Baillie Scott, "It was his proudest boast, except that he never did boast and was not at all proud, was that someone had written of his work 'he has built more houses that have done less harm to the landscape than any living architect.'" I expect that Baillie Scott's houses will survive for centuries, as long as there are craftsmen within the building industry who have developed the fundamental but not extraordinary skills necessary to preserve the quality of the original structures.

Professor James Kornwolf is perhaps the most erudite and succinct in crystallizing the contribution of Baillie Scott: "The small house was the ideal of an age where architects reminded critics, who reminded their readers, that 'the happiness of the greatest number is the best rule for modern times' and Baillie Scott's main attempt was to bring art to the small house, a thing unprecedented in the history of architecture. Given the mass, technological character of modern times, this achievement ought not to be dismissed as minor, not to say trivial. If only because housing remains at the root of the unsolved dilemmas of Modern architecture, it should be realized that Scott's work at least points the way to a new monumentality of the human spirit, if it did not attain it" (Kornwolf, p. 157). The confounding irony is that Baillie Scott was not, and is still not, recognized in his own country as a "revolutionizer of taste." Given the countless architectural atrocities executed in Great Britain (and elsewhere), perhaps it is time to finally appreciate the contribution of the leading influencer and innovator of interior planning of the twentieth century.

Ivydene

Douglas, Isle of Man, 1892–1893

Entrance facade with entry porch mimicking the rest of the facade. The stairwell's window is above the entry porch. The red sandstone is from Peel on the Isle of Man.

RIGHT *Garden facade. The windows have been changed to maximize light. They were originally leaded casement windows.*

Ivydene is Baillie Scott's earliest surviving major commission. It is also considered to be his finest and most successful house on the Isle of Man. Situated on a bluff overlooking Douglas Bay, Ivydene takes advantage of spectacular views while still being protected enough to maintain a lush garden. It was one of the first houses to be built in Little Switzerland.

Many of its details are similar to those on subsequent Baillie Scott houses. Even in this early work Baillie Scott took great pride and care in the design of every aspect of the exterior and interior. Half-timbering on top of local red Peel sandstone was unusual for the time. The entrance facade embraces visitors with a wonderful sense of shelter and protection. The intricately carved bargeboards are particularly impressive, setting Ivydene apart from houses typically seen in the south of England with its much more Celtic profile.

Baillie Scott's use of fine craftsmen is also a signature that is consistent in most of his houses. The details are exquisite and

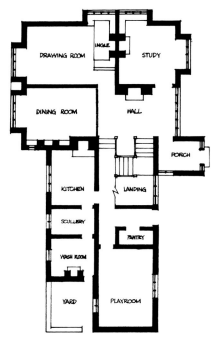

*Stairs lead up to an open room halfway up and down
to the kitchen and service area. The fine turning and
the arches are quite Victorian.*

OPPOSITE *The fluid Arts and Crafts stained glass
design on the front entry porch window anticipates
Art Nouveau style, which became popular after 1895.*

FOLLOWING PAGES *Living room with inglenook.
Fireplace with copper repoussé fire hood design is
attributed to Archibald Knox. The ingle becomes
a room within a room, and here is the first of many
fire surrounds using Delft tile.*

the carvings in Ivydene are some of the finest works of art in the
Arts and Crafts movement and attributed to Skinner & Clarke.
The design of the copper repoussé fire hood in the living room
is attributed to Archibald Knox, who went on to become one of
the iconic designers for Liberty & Co.

Heart motifs appear in most of Baillie Scott's houses and have
been modified and partially hidden over time. The architect's
extraordinary, near ubiquitous use of this motif derives from Victorian Romanticism, something Baillie Scott never relinquished.
C. F. A. Voysey is also associated with hearts in his designs and
interiors, but his use was not as fresh and innovative as Baillie
Scott's.

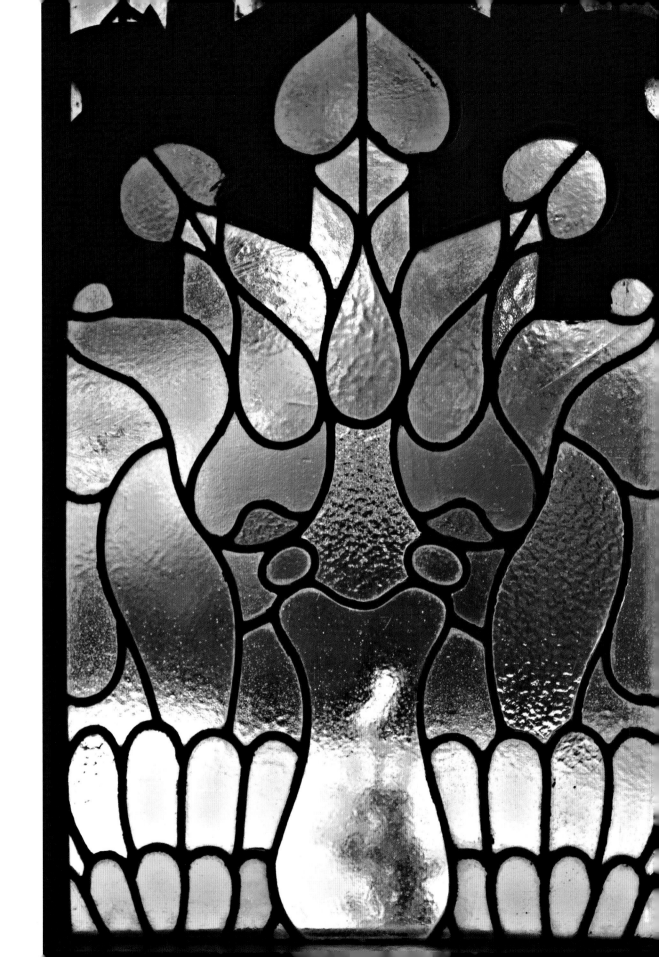

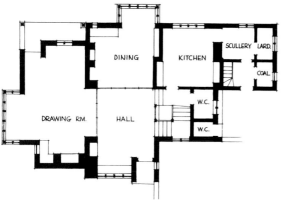

Red House

Douglas, Isle of Man, 1892–1893

Red House was designed by and for Baillie Scott, who for ten years occupied this fresh and innovative structure. Influenced by Kentish houses with hanging tiles, the initial design was unfamiliar on the Isle of Man. All of the materials were imported, surely causing a stir at the time. During his time on the Isle of Man, Baillie Scott designed and completed only eight houses there.

The interior is especially noteworthy for being even bolder than the interior at Ivydene. Here Baillie Scott designed partitions that allow the living room and the dining room to open into the hall, an idea that came from the interior planning of the Shingle Style but which he took further to allow for the transformation of a large contiguous space into smaller intimate spaces with specific functions. Along with Ivydene, Red House established Baillie Scott as a visionary who understood the value of perceived space in a relatively small structure and the potential to create multiple uses out of the same space.

ABOVE LEFT *The font style of the date is firmly Arts and Crafts. The gargoyle is both terrifying and terrified, a paradoxical design, hard to achieve.*

ABOVE MIDDLE *A stylized stained glass window in the dining room.*

OPPOSITE *Entrance facade with a combination of red brick and intricate half-timbering on gable. The massive chimney is Jacobean in feel and serves three rooms.*

FOLLOWING PAGES *West facade with formal garden in foreground. The simple lines of the hanging tile are reminiscent of both Kentish vernacular and Shingle Style.*

Oakleigh

Douglas, Isle of Man, 1893–1894

LEFT *The entry porch of Oakleigh features more simply carved bargeboards than Ivydene and Red House.*

RIGHT *The garden facade.*

Oakleigh is the house designed by Baillie Scott that particularly refers back to the Shingle Style, with its hanging tiles, verandah, and awnings. Ironically the house is also particularly English, with the front entry porch and hanging tiles common in many parts of the south. Oakleigh was commissioned by one of Baillie Scott's builders, W. Macadam.

One unique feature in the design for Oakleigh is the octagonal bay windows, which in combination resemble a tower. The windows are remarkably large for a Baillie Scott house, almost spanning the distance from floor to ceiling. The half-timbering and carved bargeboards on the front facade pay homage to the Tudor houses from the south of England that so obviously influenced the architect.

Key features common to subsequent Baillie Scott houses are the placement of the entrance and kitchen along the front facade and the living spaces at the rear of the house. Oakleigh is sited with a view of the ocean to the south, an ideal situation for light-filled primary rooms.

The proximity of Oakleigh, Red House, and Ivydene in Little Switzerland fueled a spate of imitations, which annoyed Baillie Scott to the extent that he cited this as the reason for his departure from the Isle of Man.

24

Bexton Croft

Knutsford, Cheshire, 1894–1896

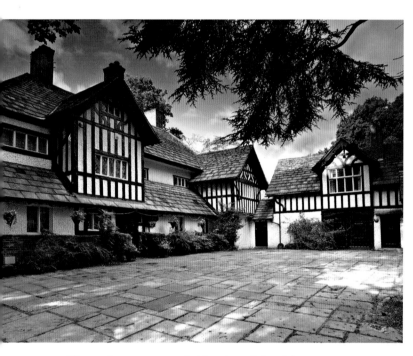

*The grand entrance courtyard with semi-attached coach house.
The terraced roof emphasizes the horizontal aspect of the facade.*

RIGHT *On the garden facade the Shingle Style is clearly visible.
The octagonal tower houses the bright living room and the master
suite above. The wing on the left is a later addition.*

Bexton Croft is the culmination of Baillie Scott's early
style; it is here he articulates his ideas very nearly perfectly. The structure is an organic flow of spaces that open
and close as the occasion requires. The flexibility of the spaces is
remarkable: all are connected but can also be closed off, with each
having two points of entry.

The great hall is the central space off of which are the drawing room and the dining room, separated on the south side by
pocket doors. This makes a heavily paneled room surprisingly
light by having all three rooms provide additional ambience.

Detail of entrance facade showing dowelled and pegged half-timbering, carved bargeboard, and irreverent face on the downpipe.

RIGHT *Extravagant medley of details on the coach house, with the strap hinges being particularly noteworthy.*

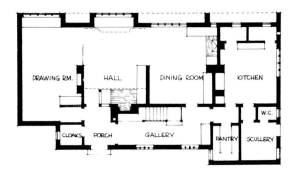

LEFT *The door handles throughout Bexton Croft are hinged.*

BELOW LEFT *Interior of Bexton Croft showing all three main rooms with hidden staircase, which leads to minstrels' gallery. Pocket doors recess to allow a great contiguous space.*

OPPOSITE *The double-height, corbel-ceilinged great hall.*

FOLLOWING PAGES *Dining room with recessed fireplace and Delft tiles. The repoussé fire hood, similar to the one at Ivydene, was made by the same craftsman in Douglas, Isle of Man.*

Bexton Croft illustrates the core difference between Baillie Scott and Frank Lloyd Wright; Baillie Scott's core is space (the great hall), while Wright's core is mass (the chimney). The house is also Baillie Scott's first foray into incorporating rescued material from older structures to give the feel of a much more mature structure. There is a delightful brass plaque in the great hall that reads: "Bexton Croft. Built in 1896 for Donald & Bessie MacPherson. Architect, M. H. Bailey Scott. Builders, John & Joseph Beswick, Bexton. Old oak paneling, stairs & doors out of St. Mary's Church, Manchester. Oak floors, hearth curbs & hall ceiling made from old timber, out of first railway carriages, which ran between Manchester & Liverpool. Door handles copied from Cwydir Castle. Door knocker from house at Poet's Corner."

Another beautifully engraved plaque, in the dining room, reads:

> Bexton Croft was lucky in having for its first tenants Two Trustful Swallows, who 'midst the noise and bustle of erection peacefully nested here.
>
> Learn then, wher'ere we are, to live aright,
> For life's uncertain as a swallow's flight,
> We come, we build, and for a season stay,
> Then into the unknown we pass away.

Leafield and Braeside

Onchan, Isle of Man, 1896–1897

This lovely terrace house, which still maintains significant presence in the neighborhood, is situated to enjoy a sweeping view of Douglas Bay. This was Baillie Scott's most successful foray into "attached houses." The terrace has a strong horizontal aspect and a relatively deep roof, which became a key feature in many of Baillie Scott's subsequent houses. The squat entry porches, with their angled buttresses, help give the building a feeling of solidity. Another key feature at Leafield and Braeside is the use of white harled roughcast to cover the entire surface of the walls, which are delightfully adorned with pebble motifs. The use of roughcast became one of Baillie Scott's hallmarks on his exterior designs until 1907.

Baillie Scott successfully completed a series of well-planned terrace houses in Little Switzerland and Falcon Cliff in Douglas that are the basis for a chapter in his book *Gardens and Houses* on small affordable housing. Here he elucidates the principles that make these spaces appear larger than they really are by employing partitions that move back to reveal a combined space that is more than the sum of its parts. The individual units are large by modern standards for a semidetached house and have a layout well suited to modern urban living.

These terrace houses led Baillie Scott to contemplate the need for first-rate interior planning in the small dwellings that were prevalent in Victorian urban life. In *Gardens and Houses* he successfully articulated designs for small houses that were far more practical than those being built at the time. Ironically the interior plans are better suited to contemporary living than the work of many architects who still create crowded spaces and demonstrate little respect for their inhabitants.

Garden faade of Leafield and Braeside.
Distinctive chimneys, inset pebble motifs,
and bay windows distinguish this
terrace house.

Rusticated and charming door details each offer distinct welcomes.

RIGHT *Entrance facade with detail of rusting gate. Proximity to the sea necessitates constant maintenance.*

Onchan Village Hall

Onchan, Isle of Man, 1897–1898

The Onchan Village Hall influenced many small municipal buildings and churches in Europe. Critics have suggested that the structure is a prime example of the serious and successful integration of both design and architecture, and that Josef Hoffmann's church at Hohenberg, Austria, was influenced by this structure. The hall has retained its original function as meeting room, theater, sports hall, and community center. Baillie Scott's use of hearts here has great impact due to the multifunctional nature of the hall.

The village hall, which pays homage to the designs of Voysey, is extremely simple, with white harled roughcast walls, a steeply sloping hipped roof, and an exquisite bell tower, all shored up by well-proportioned and spaced buttresses. Equally simple is Baillie Scott's first use of exposed beamed ceiling in the double-height hall with a stage at one end. The only embellishment is the extensive use of hearts in the windows and the intricate wrought ironwork on the exterior railings and gates.

This hall is awaiting a renovation. Remarkably, the Isle of Man's preservation codes are subject to frequent abuse, which has resulted in many significant houses being lost to new development. With such an amazing collection of the earliest Baillie Scott houses on the Isle of Man, it is a shame that there is not a greater desire there to save and fund the restoration of these remarkable buildings.

TOP *Side entrance to the hall with modern chimney and Gothic bell tower.*

MIDDLE *Hearts, hearts . . . and more hearts.*

OPPOSITE *Graceful proportions on the Parish Hall belie the interior space. The buttresses solidify the structure and the steep pitch on the long roof gives the aura of protection.*

Five Gables

Cambridge, Cambridgeshire, 1897–1898

RIGHT *The eclectic design of Five Gables features a living room bay window extruded from one corner of the house. On the right the small roof of the dining ingle can be seen.*

This small house in Cambridge is distinguished by Baillie Scott's application of a refined aesthetic to a small house. Arts and Crafts ideals imbue his design for Five Gables: while the house may be small there is no reason why it should not benefit from great design, with exceptional warmth and detail, while costing little more than an ordinary house.

Five Gables still works as a graceful and accommodating series of spaces, with the hall connecting the dining room and living room to create a contiguous space with ingles upon opening two sets of double doors. Baillie Scott's use of glass in doors and space dividers is fresh and innovative. Here he uses "bottle-bottom" glass to provide light while still retaining privacy within each room. Ornamental embellishment is extremely simple and confined to hearts in the leaded windows, repoussé firehoods, and staircase.

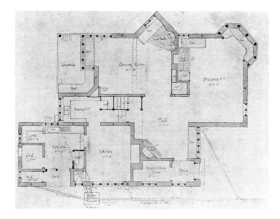

PRECEDING PAGES *Garden facade with long roof. The conservatory was a later but welcome addition that does not detract from the original design.*

LEFT *Double doors of the living room looking into the hall and up the stairs. The use of textured glass allows additional light into all of the rooms without sacrificing much privacy.*

RIGHT *Stair detail.*

BELOW RIGHT *Dining room inglenook with liberal application of hearts.*

Blackwell

*Bowness-on-Windemere, Westorland, Cumbria,
1898–1900*

*The garden facade demonstrates Baillie Scott's random window
placement, which was dictated by the interior plan and breaks
up the mass of the building.*

RIGHT *The grand front entrance to Blackwell, with sheer roughcast
walls and round chimneys, common features in the Lake District.*

The most impressive of Baillie Scott's early houses and one of the most significant, Blackwell has undergone a major renovation to bring it back from an uncertain fate to become a museum, making it the only Baillie Scott house open to the public. Blackwell was built for Sir Edward Holt, who was a wealthy brewer and the mayor of Manchester. No expense was spared, and Baillie Scott finally had a client prepared to let the young architect expand his vision by essaying a baronial mansion where he could express his ideas at a scale a little grander than that of a typical country house. Here one can see a remarkable fusion of Arts and Crafts and Art Nouveau architecture, which makes Blackwell one of the most significant houses of the turn of the twentieth century.

OPPOSITE *The larger of the bay windows of the White Room allows for commanding views of Lake Windemere and the Coniston Fells beyond. The garden is a series of terraces that allows views from any part of the grounds.*

RIGHT *The truly remarkable White Room is virtually a piece of sculpture, carved by using subtle relief of the plaster work and wood. The chair between the door and the ingle is a Baillie Scott design. The rowan tree motif is used here and throughout Blackwell.*

BELOW RIGHT *The inglenook is the mature iteration of a fireplace at Ivydene on the Isle of Man; the tiles in the fireplace are by William De Morgan; the andirons are original Baillie Scott designs that also appear at Waldbühl. The slender columns, representing trees, are the fusion of Arts and Crafts and Art Nouveau. The mirrors would have accentuated candlelight.*

FOLLOWING PAGES *The great hall is Baillie Scott's most spectacular room, and has all the key features: the inglenook with bay window, the minstrels' gallery above, the stair hall to one side, both ground-floor and first-floor corridors with window galleries that allow light into the spectacular room. The chair was designed by Baillie Scott.*

The house abounds with inglenooks and window seats to take advantage of the stunning views of Lake Windermere and the Coniston Fells beyond. Blackwell also features Baillie Scott's earliest example of a windowpane vent, later appearing in Gryt-Howe and The Tudors.

Woodcarver Arthur Simpson of Kendall created in the great hall one of the finest examples of Arts and Crafts carving in England. The wainscot running around the billiards room alcove is extraordinary, as is the bench seat recess. The pinnacle of Simpson's carving, however, is the staircase screen, which is delicate yet sturdy, and which enjoys a delightfully lifelike quality. Of the four great Baillie Scott houses where the carving is a significant detail—Ivydene, Blackwell, Waldbühl, and Ashwood Place—Blackwell's is the finest.

The three principal rooms are each successful for different reasons: the great hall manages to retain the feel of a cottage in a room whose dimensions (28 by 46 feet) are unmatched in any house of this size and of the period; the dining room has beautifully detailed paneling and Hessian wallpaper, which remarkably survives; and the monochromatic drawing room is an exquisite example of opulent restraint.

It is at Blackwell that Baillie Scott's experiments in Ivydene, Red House, and Bexton Croft can be said to have matured. For example, the master bedroom fireplace in Ivydene is too similar to the fire ingle in the drawing room at Blackwell to be mere coincidence. The interior plan is a successful refinement of Red House, though the exterior, particularly the east garden facade, has been criticized for the irregularity of the fenestration.

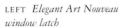

LEFT *Elegant Art Nouveau window latch*

BELOW LEFT *Detail of Arthur Simpson's exquisite carving, demonstrating his understanding of wood, here quarter-sawn oak producing remarkable ambiguity as these leaves also resemble feathers.*

RIGHT *The Hessian wallpaper in the dining room is distinguished by its state of preservation. Significant Arts and Crafts furniture sits under a corbelled ceiling similar to that at Bexton Croft.*

FOLLOWING PAGES
Left: Stained-glass window in the White Room with tulips and birds rendered in Baillie Scott's unmistakable style. Right: Detail of the dining ingle.

FIRST FLOOR PLAN

White Lodge

Wantage, Oxfordshire, 1898–1899

White Lodge is undoubtedly the first of Baillie Scott's houses demonstrating his signature exterior style. The sheer mass of the walls, combined with minimal overhanging eaves, long rooflines, and a far more linear and sculptural feel than anything seen previously make a strong argument for White Lodge being the first truly modern house, and undoubtedly it influenced Charles Rennie Mackintosh, Frank Lloyd Wright, and the larger European architectural community, among them Adolf Loos (Kornwolf, p. 193).

White Lodge differs from Baillie Scott's previous houses for the following reasons: the windows' exterior sills are as shallow as possible to create the appearance of an even surface; the punctuation of the fenestration is now quite linear; the exterior walls are entirely roughcast with no embellishment whatsoever; there are minimal eaves, so creating crisp edges; and the house has much more pleasing proportions. The long roofline that descends to encompass the garden entrance porch is an extremely elegant solution and, when viewed in combination with the chimney, reveals Baillie Scott's evolving grasp of minimalism and function.

The interior planning is much the same as in his previous designs, with exceptional circulation and detailing. The main

Garden facade showing Baillie Scott at his innovative best. The modernism of this design is groundbreaking with the roof falling beautifully over the porch entrance, breaking the mass and creating intimacy. The chimneys become modern columns extending into the sky.

LEFT *View into the dining room from the living room. The woodwork was originally painted white.*

BELOW LEFT *The living room fireplace is completely intact with repoussé fire hood, Deflt tiles, and original red quarry tile on the floor.*

OPPOSITE *Study fireplace and bench seat with an abundance of heart details.*

LEFT *Stained-glass details and copper door plates, similar to those at Blackwell and Five Gables.*

OPPOSITE *Left: The magical stained-glass window in the ingle of the living room is firmly planted in Baillie Scott's Arts and Crafts idiom, with forward-looking intimations of Art Nouveau and even Art Deco styles.*
Right: Open stair hall off the living room. The simplicity of the newel posts reflects the simplicity of the chimney columns. The graphic leaf motif breaks up the sheer massing of the balustrade.

rooms on the ground floor have remained essentially untouched. It was designed as a residence for the chaplain of St. Mary's Convent and has been a residence at the convent ever since. There is a simple but not austere feel, with the signature heart motif contributing a softening effect. The repoussé fire hoods are exquisite, and it is all the more remarkable that there are three in consecutive rooms, and all in outstanding condition.

The now hallmark Baillie Scott stained glass, a unique fusion of fluid Art Nouveau and minimalist Arts and Crafts influences, is used appropriately throughout White Lodge.

White House

Helensburgh, Scotland, 1898–1900

LEFT *The garden facade is distinguished by sheer massing, modern chimneys, and orderly fenestration. The dimensions of the window to the great hall (second in from the right) originally extended up to the second story, which the current owners intend to restore.*

ABOVE *The entrance facade of White House demonstrates Baillie Scott's innovative minimalism. In a manner similar to Blackwell, the interior planning dictates the wall punctuation and window placement.*

Baillie Scott was at the height of his inventiveness when he designed the White House. Elemental but not oversimplified, the White House makes innovation look easy: minimal eave overhang; windows that cleanly puncture the walls to create a geometric, cubist structure; and superlative interior planning demonstrate Baillie Scott's remarkable stylistic integrity. The white roughcast treatment of the walls enhances the whole and catapults the structure well into the twentieth

GROUND FLOOR PLAN

RIGHT *View in from the octagonal bay window.*

century. Baillie Scott tightens the looser arrangement of the windows at Blackwell and integrates the interior free plan with a more formal consideration of the exterior.

It is generally accepted within academic circles that Mackintosh, who had access to many of Baillie Scott's plans, looked closely at the White House before designing the Hill House a mere two hundred yards further up the hill in Helensburgh a couple of years later. There are many cues and more importantly a sensibility that did not exist before the White House and White Lodge.

The fenestration has been altered from the original, and the great hall has been converted into two rooms. The current owners are undertaking a sympathetic renovation and intend to restore the great hall.

Castletown Police Station

Castletown, Isle of Man, 1900–1902

Baillie Scott's last commission on the Isle of Man, before he set himself free on mainland England, is perfectly set into its surroundings while still retaining its Arts and Crafts identity. Rushen Castle in the background is a significant thirteenth-century structure, and the police station detracts nothing from the historic castle but exists harmoniously with all of the other buildings in the vicinity. The site, with an existing house, was selected by a special committee and was purchased for 300 pounds.

Baillie Scott made a point of using a limited repertoire of materials and forms to create this harmony. The cylindrical corner reflects the round gatehouse of the castle, merely feet away. It appears to be a building that is associated with the castle and of the era but for some clever introduction of Arts and Crafts aesthetics: with the curve of the north gable, the proximity of the east gable and chimney to the rounded corner, and, of course, the classic Arts and Crafts text carved into the masonry.

The police station still functions exactly as intended, which says much for the quality of life in Castletown as well as Baillie Scott's practical design: the only additions are electricity and a few computers. The doors and hardware resonate with those of the castle without sacrificing any expression of Baillie Scott's idiom; for instance, his gable over the entrance is a classic Arts and Crafts flourish.

Castletown Police Station is well integrated into its environment and complements Castle Rushen in the background.

Danestream

Milford on Sea, Lymington, Hampshire, 1904

Danestream is an important house in the Baillie Scott canon. Images were published in his 1906 *Houses and Gardens*. It is easy to see the progression from Blackwell to White Lodge, then White House, and finally to Danestream.

Professor Kornwolf could not find this house on his odyssey among Baillie Scott's houses in 1970, though he would have loved to. According to Kornwolf it is one of Baillie Scott's most remarkable designs for a small house. The arrangement of the rooms is unique: the front door opens onto a passage, which leads directly through to the garden, separating the study and living room and thus creating an open corridor around which the house is organized. The rooms here are well proportioned but do not interconnect. The diagonal flow is remarkable and extends from small cubby-holed rooms housing bicycles and the larder to the kitchen then to a larger dining room and through the open corridor to the living room. Danestream is smaller than White Lodge and White House but is no less comfortable.

Like White House and White Lodge, Danestream has sheer roughcast walls, flush windows, minimal eave overhang, and the resulting crisp edges. Dramatic steep pitched roofs exaggerate the impression of shelter and come tantalizingly close to the ground. The geometric and austere treatment of the chimney is also reminiscent of White Lodge, but due to the smaller scale of the house appears that much more bold. The two arched doorways on either side of the open corridor provide the only relief to the otherwise entirely angular exterior.

The entrance facade at Danestream is a continuation of the innovation seen at Blackwell, White House, and White Lodge, but in a condensed form. The front door opens onto a passage that leads through the house to the garden and separates the study and living room from the dining room, kitchen, and service rooms.

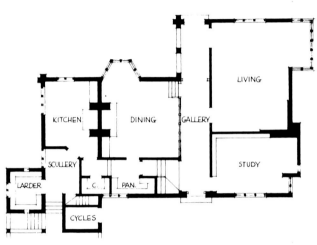

Danestream's west facade, showing the sheer simple mass of the chimney as the predominant architectural feature shrouded by the roof.

LIVING

KITCHEN
DINING
GALLERY

SCULLERY

STUDY

LARDER
C.
PAN.

CYCLES

Dove's Nest

Uckfield, East Sussex, 1904

The eclectic massing on the entrance facade of Dove's Nest, with stepped-back gables, unique entry porch roof, and stair tower, achieve's an intimate, unimposing profile.

RIGHT *Kitchen garden and irregular fenestration*

Originally called Crow's Nest, this gem is isolated in Ashdown Forest and is now appropriately used as a spiritual retreat. The exterior is organic, with the fenestration revealing internal use. The front entrance roof is uniquely offset to a corner of the drive facade, giving a casual air to the structure, while the curve of the buttress sweeps the eye to the three gabled roofs.

Dove's Nest is remarkable for the amount and variety of stained glass and stands out among houses from Baillie Scott's early period in this regard. The rooms flow beautifully and are now used individually for small meditation groups or are opened up to accommodate bigger functions. The inglenook in the

Garden facade with bay window that echoes the triangular entry-porch roof.

living room is particularly fine and encompasses all that Baillie Scott felt was important about creating intimate spaces within larger rooms.

Dove's Nest was built at the same time as Baillie Scott's house in America, which to date has not been identified. The plans were quite similar, and it is widely believed that the house would look similar to Dove's Nest. However, the house in America is the only house where Baillie Scott extended the windows three floors in the extruding bays.

Dove's Nest is an extremely important house not only of Baillie Scott's career but also of the period because so much of the interior and exterior is intact. This is a testament to the vision of the director of the retreat center, who during the early 1970s embarked on a journey similar to Kornwolf's search for Baillie Scott's legacy.

Stained glass combining flower and heart motifs.

RIGHT *The living room ingle is an intimate, self-contained
room within a room in pure Baillie Scott style.*

FOLLOWING PAGES *Left: Front entry hallway.
Right: The built-in closet, clerestory windows, and eclectic paint
combination give this bedroom a modern feel a century after completion.*

*Pages 82–83: The stained-glass window in the wall dividing
the hall from the living room is reminiscent of the glass at Blackwell.*

Tanglewood

Letchworth, Hertfordshire, 1906–1907

*Tanglewood's asymmetrical yet remarkably balanced
entrance facade and the more informal garden facade.*

Tanglewood was originally designed for the Letchworth Garden City, part of the movement to change the Victorian paradigm of crowded urban living and all its associated social ills by creating cities that were deliberately designed to promote healthy living. The movement floundered but left a legacy of pleasant urban/suburban centers within commuting distance to London. Built for a craftsman, Tanglewood is a modest but comfortable house with a large main room. The bedrooms are relatively small-scaled, as they tended to be in middle-class households at the turn of the twentieth century. The lot is modest as well but provides the necessary privacy while retaining proximity to neighbors and easy access to the city

Tanglewood is easily identifiable as one of the architect's creations but it still manages to maintain a unique identity. Baillie Scott in this phase of his career was veering toward the picturesque, and this can be seen on the front facade, where the roofs on either side of the entrance try to reach the ground. The influence of medieval farmhouses on the architect and can readily be seen at Tanglewood: small, irregular openings for the windows and the half-timbered treatment on the entry recess show Baillie Scott's move away from his modern idiom.

Bill House

Selsey, West Sussex, 1906–1907

Covered passageway into the courtyard with motor carriage house and viewing tower.

Right: View of Bill House's entrance facade from the tower. Bill House was deliberately built on the waterfront to prevent any development in front of it. The decorative pattern of the courtyard cobblestones frames the front entrance path.

Built for Byron Peters on a beachfront site, Bill House possesses many of the most innovative attributes of a typical Baillie Scott house. Though it appears deceptively small from the garden facade, Bill House features a great hall and spacious bedrooms along the garden facade, while the smaller rooms tucked under the roof enjoy plenty of light. A covered passageway leads to a courtyard composed of local sea pebbles. The house's tower structure maintains a spectacular and unobstructed view out to sea and during World War II was used by the Coast Guard as a lookout. The rear elevation emphasizes the house's horizontal profile with one long steeply pitched roof punctuated by two gables at either end. The front facade is composed of a more intricate series of gables and dormer windows.

The sun loggia on Bill House's garden facade has been fenestrated. The great hall is on the left hand side, and the flat dormer window roof on the right appears intended to minimize the asymmetry, drawing the eye to the two dormer windows with gables balanced directly above the three arches of the loggia.

Baillie Scott's interior plan is somewhat unusual due to the location of the master bedroom on the ground floor at the eastern end of the house. The bright double-height hall at the western end creates a delightful cruciform configuration that contains a dining recess. The loggia is central to the design of Bill House and successfully maintains an Italian approach to circulation: the front and back doors are directly linked by the corridor that connects both wings of the house. While most of Bill House is covered in roughcast, here Baillie Scott used a variety of materials: wood for the tower, chalk and marble for the loggia, and seashells, lapis, and onyx for the checkers above the loggia and main entrance gable, exemplifying Baillie Scott's divergence from his austere, entirely roughcast exteriors toward a more romantic ideal, softening the exteriors by introducing varied materials and creating an overtly picturesque feel.

Waldbühl

Uzwil, Switzerland, 1907–1911

A tree-lined avenue on the right leads into the circular entry courtyard of Waldbühl.

RIGHT *The grand front entrance evokes the client's dream of the ideal English country house.*

FOLLOWING PAGES *The symmetrical garden facade abounds with detail. The tile on the fountain, the stair risers, and the wall of the terrace are of the same pattern as that at Sanford Cottage, Dundee, Scotland. This courtyard was originally designed to be a rose garden but was grassed over to allow the children to play closer to the house.*

Waldbühl is the most fascinating of Baillie Scott's houses and his undisputed masterpiece. An English country house in the heart of Switzerland, it is still in the finest condition and is the only house designed by Baillie Scott that is still in the possession of the original client's family, with the current owner having lived here since 1939. Here the architect was finally able to design all aspects of the house—the exterior, interior, and garden—to his exacting standards and completely in line with his pioneering vision. He was at the height of his innovative creativity when he designed Waldbühl, which remains a testament to Baillie Scott's maturity.

The pool is original to the house design and has been used faithfully every summer.

RIGHT *The site, with a view of the distant Alps, originally had few trees.*

Waldbühl represents a great collaboration between architect and client: Theodor Bühler was an engineer and progressive, a perfect match for the innovative architect. Their complete correspondence is preserved in the Waldbühl archive and is invaluable as almost all of Baillie Scott's plans and designs have been destroyed. Bühler, an Anglophile from his days as a student in England, was determined to re-create the ideal English country house, and Waldbühl's exquisite craftsmanship was the result of collaboration and extensive effort made by English artisans who were seconded to Switzerland to install the marble and paneling. The metalwork was crafted by the Artificer's Guild of London, and the curtains, slipcovers, and wall hangings were fabricated by E. Hunter of Letchworth.

Baillie Scott also designed all furniture for the house, which was made by John P. White of Pyglie Works and which has been slowly repatriated beginning in 1939 as part of a remarkable labor of love to re-create the feel of the original house.

The exterior is laid out in a classic L shape with the primary rooms facing south and an extensive service wing along the east facade with multiple bedrooms for servants, an arrangement that

PRECEDING PAGES *The service wing of Waldbühl—with seven servants' bedrooms—on a foggy September morning.*

ABOVE *The protected loggia on the east side of the house is a comfortable outdoor room.*

he often replicated after 1906. All of the windows on the ground level have thick internal shutters made of quartersawn oak. Most of the material was imported from England at considerable cost.

The lightness of the "ladies'" drawing room is remarkable. The suite of furniture, plasterwork, and silk wallpaper is easily the most impressive of any of Baillie Scott's rooms, which is quite a feat considering that two rooms away is the dining room with remarkable inlay and marquetry, original Tiffany lamps, and a unique Baillie Scott dining table and chairs.

The gardens are still laid out as first executed except for the lawns, which were originally a rose garden long since replaced

after countless scrapes and too many tears. Much of the intended garden plan was never realized, being too ambitious for the needs of the family and also because Theodor died prematurely in 1915 before the garden could be completed.

Scott's dependence upon color in his interiors, nearly always in conjunction with elegant, simple patterns derived from animal and vegetable forms, impressed Hermann Muthesius, Adolf Loos, and others critical of individual expression in art. By 1904, Baillie Scott's precise articulation of formal principles had led not to self-indulgence or expressionism but to a new and universally applicable approach to domestic architecture.

The former flower room on the opposite side of the house is now a quiet indoor garden oasis.

FOLLOWING PAGES *The main hall with its original furniture is an extraordinary Arts and Crafts room. Baillie Scott plays with ceiling height in the entry foyer, which opens up to the grand room. Heavy oak internal shutters are opened and closed every day by Frau Bühler, a twenty-minute workout. The great hall leads into the "ladies'" drawing room with its crystal-paned doors.*

TOP *Baillie Scott's chandelier complements the incredibly detailed plasterwork.*

ABOVE *Detail of inlaid Art Nouveau motif on the music cabinet in the "ladies'" drawing room.*

RIGHT *In the "ladies'" drawing room the furniture is unique to this room and fully demonstrates what Baillie Scott was capable of doing when given the opportunity. The craftsmanship is extraordinary and Baillie Scott's furniture aesthetic even more so. The silk wall fabric matches the plasterwork above the picture rail. The marble fireplace has three flower mosaics with inlaid mother-of-pearl and abalone. Color plays a leading role in this room in contrast to the traditional Arts and Crafts hall.*

FOLLOWING PAGES *Dining room with inlaid wood paneling and built-in sideboards. The paneling for the dining room and the study was executed by Bailey's of London under careful supervision by Baillie Scott. The dining room table and chairs were also designed by Baillie Scott, and the Tiffany lamps were bought for the house at the time of construction.*

PRECEDING PAGES *The study mimics an old English paneled room with Pugin-style paneling above the fireplace and intricately carved ceiling panels. A magnolia-patterned lamp by Tiffany sits on the desk Baillie Scott specifically purchased for the room.*

OPPOSITE *Whimsical andirons in the upstairs morning room.*

RIGHT *The master bedroom is a delightfully cozy room, with a beautifully plastered barrel-vaulted ceiling and delicately painted panel detailing in a unique Scottish-Swiss style. The king-size bed is unusually large for the Arts and Crafts movement; on one of his three visits, Baillie Scott deemed the bed unsatisfactory, so it was returned to England to be remade!*

BELOW RIGHT *The master bathroom is the only extant original Baillie Scott bathroom. The sidetable is also a Baillie Scott design.*

Longburton House

Longburton, Sherbourne, Dorset, 1908–1909

Longburton House, formerly known as Burton Court, is remarkable for its use of recycled material. Almost the entire structure was salvaged from abandoned country houses. The feel of Longburton House is ancient; the panels designed by Gothic Revivalist A. W. N. Pugin and the carvings on the staircase are obviously much older than any Arts and Crafts details could be; throughout the house there is too much authentic patina.

Baillie Scott assembled a country mansion that feels like it has been around for centuries. The beams are ancient and the stone mantles are positively massive. The original plans were even more elaborate than the realized scheme and were scaled down significantly by the client—the cost of assembling a jigsaw puzzle of a house like this was higher than new construction.

Longburton House did not earn Baillie Scott much critical praise, and the interior plan is not as fresh as his earlier, more open plans. The goal here was to deceive the viewer into thinking that the house was older than it is, and Baillie Scott coined the term Jacobean for this type of house.

Longburton House is now undergoing renovations on the pathways and is situated on a working farm.

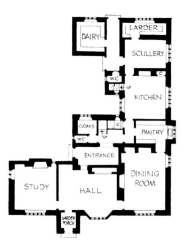

TOP *This delightful key is one of three in the house with a heart motif; the door handle is one half of a heart and the latch plate another.*

RIGHT *The main living room features antique paneling, a massive beamed ceiling, and recycled stone floors.*

White Cottage

Harrow, Middlesex, 1908

White Cottage's irregularity on the eastern or entrance facade is accounted for by the wish to preserve an old tree and to form a courtyard around it. The tree has gone, but the courtyard creates an intimate oasis that passersby can enjoy. The cottage directly abuts the road and is one of Baillie Scott's least private houses. Originally the walls would have been entirely harled roughcast, as Baillie Scott railed against the cheap addition of obviously added planking to imitate half-timbering. The interior planning is a culmination of the best ideas from Baillie Scott's previous houses. The entrance hall leads to different areas of the house: to the immediate left is the private study, followed by a reception room, which also opens into the living room, then the stair room, and finally on the right the entrance to the kitchen.

White Cottage was designed for a Swiss musician, Alfred Bussweiler, and the living room is especially noteworthy for spanning the entire width of the cottage, with a music recess and a dining recess on either side. Bussweiler often entertained guests with recitals, for which this space was the perfect venue. This is one of the finest examples of a dining recess taking the place of the dining room, and Baillie Scott preserves a sense of intimacy here with the low ceilings.

When White Cottage was photographed, the new owners had yet to decorate the living room, giving the opportunity to demonstrate Baillie Scott's belief that "the room as left by the builder before it is inhabited at all, is already more than half furnished" (Kornwolf, p. 112). Cleared of day-to-day furniture, this room can seat at least eighteen people.

White Cottage was originally built around a tree in the courtyard, which has now been replaced by a fountain. The courtyard gate leads directly onto a busy sidewalk and invites passersby to look in.

114

The expansive living room features a stage for music performances and exemplifies Baillie Scott's ability to decorate a room before any furniture is placed in it.

OPPOSITE PAGE *The exquisitely plastered barrel-vaulted ceiling in the main bathroom. In the bay window is a stained glass medallion by Florence Cramm.*

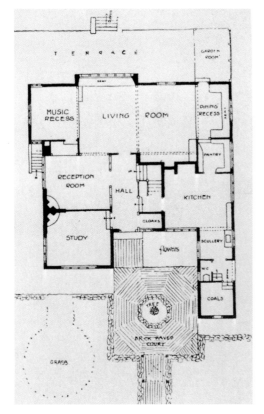

This great room is interesting. His *Houses and Gardens* was published in 1906, and this room exemplifies creating a house as if it were built up from a one-room cottage. At White Cottage the scale is small and the satellite rooms serve the whole house well. Baillie Scott railed against the scaling of a mansion down to that of a small house, creating a cramped rabbit warren of rooms.

There are three exceptional pieces of commissioned stained glass in White Cottage credited to Florence Camm working for the studio of T. W. Camm. Two reside in the music stage recess and the third is beautifully placed in the bay alcove in the elaborately plastered and barrel-vaulted bathroom.

Undershaw

Guilford, Surrey, 1908–1909

The design of this house is less revolutionary than White House or White Lodge but still defies pigeonholing. It is thoroughly modern while still constructed of Baillie Scott's well-articulated materials and with details of extremely high quality. The detailing on the brick chimney with inlaid flint on one seam and the repoussé lead gutter are such carefully crafted elements that make Baillie Scott's houses much more than the sum of their parts.

The steep hillside upon which the house is built offers spectacular views but necessitated a dwelling organized on multiple, descending levels. The sequence of rooms arranged among the house's six levels demonstrate an ingenious use of space and connectors. This beautifully planned house has been converted into two dwelling units, but the original interior shows Baillie Scott at his best. Kornwolf writes about the "houseplace," or hall, glowingly, admiring the generous access from this hub to the porch, stair, kitchen, front entrance, dining alcove, "bower," or living room, and study.

The lushly planted garden frames the path that leads down to the trellised entrance of Undershaw.

118

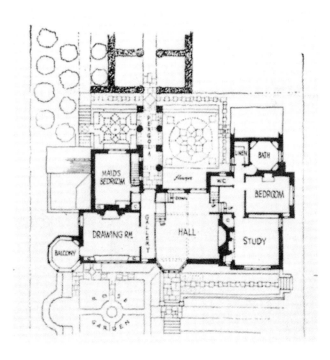

RIGHT *The garden facade has remained untouched except for the fenestration on the loggia on the left.*

ABOVE LEFT *View into the great hall from the master bedroom.*

ABOVE RIGHT *A staircase with intricately carved newel posts leads up to the master bedroom at the end of the landing.*

RIGHT *Master bedroom alcove with viewing window to the great hall, original built-in closet, and unusual strap hinges unique to Undershaw.*

OPPOSITE *The great hall is the hub that leads to the garden on the right, to the front door on the near left, and upstairs on the far left. The master bedroom viewing window can be seen on the far wall.*

Waterlow Court

Hampstead Garden Suburb, London, 1908–1909

Waterlow Court was initially built to accommodate fifty single working women in individual flats of three to four rooms, and is probably the most successful of Baillie Scott's essays in the Arts and Crafts ideal of providing the most adequate living space to working classes in the most efficient space possible, all while giving the impression of ownership by a much more affluent clientele. Baillie Scott's approach embodies the socialist ideal taken to a realistic and human level, which raises those less fortunate to a higher level and demonstrates the architect's respect for every level of society.

In *Houses and Gardens* Baillie Scott expounds his rationale:

The house of a civilized people should convey something more than the callous commercialism of the speculative builder, and should be arranged on some better principle than that which merely aims at crowding as many as possible into a given space. In this matter, the savage who decks his primitive dwelling with brightly painted carving is more advanced than we, and of all the habitations of man, surely none have quite reached such an expression of sordid meanness as the modern street of modern villa residences.

Here then is a persuasive example of allowing dignity to those who had no other choice than to live communally. The communal dining hall and sitting room allowed for socializing and helped by having communal meals that otherwise would have been much time and space wasted for the residents of the fifty dwellings had they prepared meals for themselves individually. The materials used are not as high quality as in other commissions but they are honest and have lasted well.

View of the courtyard and common dining and sitting rooms from the open-galleried entrance corridor.

124

LEFT *Cloistered walkways surround the central courtyard and protect inhabitants accessing the staircases that lead to each flat on the upper stories.*

ABOVE *Carved heart detail on newel post. Entry doors have strap hinges used on many of Baillie Scott's houses.*

Waterlow Court is a remarkable structure with exemplary circulation. The covered entrance corridor leads to the main building, and the cloister leads around on all sides to the main hall and common sitting room. No architect of his era matched Baillie Scott in the realization of making small dwellings pleasant places to live, making him the ultimate advocate for the working and middle classes as well as their finest illusionist, managing to make much out of little.

King's Close

Biddenham, Bedfordshire, 1909

B aillie Scott's lack of rapport with the inhabitants of the city of Bedford is confirmed by the fact that he received no commissions in town during his twelve years of practice there, which is rather startling, and only very few commissions for small cottages in the surrounding villages of Bedfordshire. King's Close is almost identical to Tanglewood, Letchworth, which itself begs the question whether the client specifically requested the facsimile or whether the scheme was duplicated for expediency's sake.

Even though this is a small house, attention to the needs of the occupants was not ignored. Of particular note is the banister, with a whimsical carving on the newel post, which ingeniously unbolts to allow the passage of large pieces of furniture to the upstairs bedrooms. Such details demonstrate Baillie Scott's "golden rule" for architects:

"Never construct for other people dwellings you are not prepared to live in yourself."

White Cottage

Biddenham, Bedfordshire, 1909

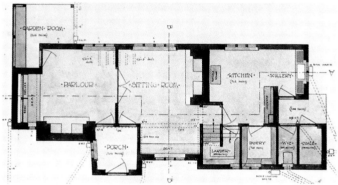

TOP *The nearly symmetrical garden facade is unusual for the architect due to the use of wooden windows.*

RIGHT *The entrance facade of White Cottage, Biddenham, shows Baillie Scott in full command of the small cottage aesthetic, fitting in well with this beautiful village while still retaining the unmistakable Baillie Scott signature long sloping roofs and perfect proportions.*

Very close to King's Close in the same charming village of Biddenham is White Cottage. Though the house is almost entirely sheathed in harled roughcast, Baillie Scott still manages to impart his style with steeply pitched gable roofs almost reaching the ground and strap hinges on the front door. The windows are a departure from the norm: most of the architect's houses have leaded windows but White Cottage's are exclusively wooden, evidence of a restricted budget.

The cottage is diminutive but features a well-planned interior, where elm is employed almost exclusively for the doors, further indicating a much lower budget. The garden room has since been enclosed, adding to the interior space and improving circulation by connecting the dining and living rooms.

130

Windmill House

Sidmouth, Dorset, 1909

A wisteria-covered trellis leads to the entry porch.

RIGHT *Charming flint walls on the garden facade are covered in ivy, disguising the remarkably spacious interior.*

This wonderful house, formerly Home Orchard, is in the coastal town of Sidmouth in Dorset, distinguished by its Georgian and Regency architecture. The "modest" five-bedroom house has a familiarly brilliant interior layout, and it has been lovingly restored by the current owners, and the enhanced garden is one of the most intimate in the Baillie Scott collection.

The house is now covered in ivy, but underneath is a combination of stone, flint, and brick. A Yorkstone terrace runs the entire length of the garden facade, with one central staircase leading to the lawn. An additional staircase on the north side leads to a pergola covering another Yorkstone path that runs along much of the length of the northern boundary. Secluded from the road, the long pedestrian approach commences at a delightful lych-gate and follows a pathway through colorful borders.

LEFT *The trellised walkway has been lovingly restored, while the planting demonstrates the more hospitable environment of the southwest coast.*

ABOVE *Stained glass detail on the entry porch.*

The house's steeply pitched roof disguises its spacious interior. The sunroom, as in most other Baillie Scott houses, has been enclosed but still has an airy feel and improves the interior circulation of the house.

The interior spaces are exceptionally well planned, with the principle reception rooms and bedrooms benefiting from views over the gardens to the wooded hills across the Sid Valley. The living and dining rooms are divided by a pair of sliding doors and combine to create a superb entertaining space. The remarkable built-in storage contributes to the sense of spaciousness in the principle rooms by eliminating the need for cumbersome furniture. The architect also incorporated built-in storage under the eaves on the entire sleeping floor.

The plan flows in classic Baillie Scott style. Doors open and close as the occasion fits, and with all doors opened one gains the impression of being in a very large space. No other architect of his era had the ability to provide so much space in what would ordinarily appear to be a small dwelling.

Manderville

Hoddesdon, Herfordshire, 1909

Detail of the extraordinary brickwork.

RIGHT *The massive facade is modulated by extruded wings,
additional detailing on the lead flashing, and Latin script
on the gutters, similar to Undershaw and Home Close.*

Perhaps the house designed by Baillie Scott with the most
use of brick, Manderville is a large house with a nearly
symmetrical entrance facade and a massive garden facade.
Even with three prominent gables the house manages to retain a
strong horizontal aspect thanks to the presence of two garden
rooms on either side.

The brickwork is exceptional, with the courses rising over the
curved windows and merging perfectly straight again a few
courses higher. The use of quartersawn oak is extensive on the
interior. The rooms are laid out in the usual manner, with the
living and dining rooms interconnected with large paneled double doors and free access to the terrace. The carved newel posts
are almost identical to those in Undershaw, and the carved heart
dropping from the upper newel post is a feature seen at Waterlow Court and Ashwood Place.

LEFT *Baillie Scott emphasizes the structure's horizontal profile through long lines of casement windows, two low rooms on either side of the facade, and long roofs leading to them.*

ABOVE *Window latch also seen in Blackwell and White Cottage, Harrow.*

FOLLOWING PAGES *Left: Shallow Tudor arches frame details on the newel posts similar to Undershaw's. Right : Unusual bracket details in the living room.*

Home Close

Sibford Ferris, Banbury, Oxfordshire, 1910

For Home Close, an imposing house in the small village of Sibford Ferris, Baillie Scott used local building materials and integrated the house well into its environment by adapting vernacular architectural styles. With Court Lodge, Longburton House, and Home Close, Baillie Scott became stylistically anonymous in favor of designing new dwellings as "old buildings." Kornwolf writes:

> He found Banbury a place where "more than elsewhere, it seems impossible to do otherwise than follow the local building tradition." The building of this particular house gave him unusual pleasure, for there was, he tells us, "no building line decreed by blind authority"; thus the house was built close to the street and to existing buildings, which, together with Scott's house, "combine in an unpremeditated and admired disorder." The result is both pleasant and natural. Scott took full advantage of the opportunity to site his building flexibly.

The original owner modified Baillie Scott's plans and elected to keep the interior as simple as possible by foregoing extraneous embellishment. The exterior, however, is distinguished by fine details similar to those used at Blackwell.

Proposed modifications (drawn by Diane Haigh, a published expert on the architect, who renovated 48 Storey's Way to exacting standards that Baillie Scott would have appreciated) allow a much improved flow to the house and it is a shame that at the time of printing the modifications have not been executed. Local planners, for whom Baillie Scott had little time, have caused this house to be kept in a state of disrepair by refusing to allow the modifications. With modern living, every Baillie Scott kitchen and service area has been altered, and undoubtedly the architect would have designed differently had he been working today. It is thanks to Baillie Scott's understanding and use of local material and mastery of high-quality craftsmanship that Home Close will shine again once bureaucracy has been reasoned with.

The entrance facade, set back from the road, rarely sees the sun.

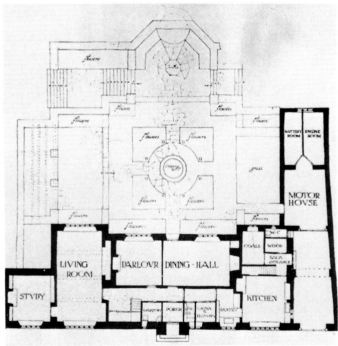

TOP *Garage door with massive hinges and inset entry door.*

RIGHT *The secluded garden awaits restoration.*

48 Storey's Way

Cambridge, Cambridgeshire, 1911

Of all the houses Baillie Scott designed in Cambridge, 48 Storey's Way, originally designed for H. A. Roberts, is perhaps the greatest example of his organically developed style. Many of his houses were designed for academics who were not necessarily wealthy but who understood the architect's brilliance for practical design and his ability to make a limited space feel large.

From the front entrance, 48 Storey's Way appears to be a relatively small house due to the long and steeply pitched roof covering half of the front facade. The long sloping roof is an important design element in many of Baillie Scott's houses: it exaggerates the horizontal profile and enhances the impression of shelter. Additionally, the architect's sense of scale makes even large structures feel intimate.

On the garden facade the true scale of the house appears. It is simple and unimposing in its exterior detail but fits well into its context. The garden adheres to the original layout, and is an intimate series of outdoor spaces.

48 Storey's Way was subject to an extensive restoration in the early 1990s by Diane Haigh. The current owners have an eclectic art collection, which complements the Arts and Crafts style admirably. The interior planning is classic Baillie Scott with great form, function, and fluidity. The stairwell becomes a hall room that features the first appearance of his iconic newel posts, which subsequently appear in Havisham House, Pilgrims, The Gatehouse, Kintail Manor, The Tudors, and Great Wood. The stairs follow his familiar "U" pattern, with landings every few steps, the practical application of which was to prevent serious falls. Baillie Scott also employed here the typical northern corridor that accesses the south-facing bedrooms, with the ergonomically sound placement of the upstairs corridor under the sloping roof.

Shaped yew trees frame the unimposing entrance.

146

Restored to the original plan, pergolas edge the first of a series of exterior rooms, which become progressively more rustic.

RIGHT *A modern sculpture offers a dramatic contrast to the house's garden facade.*

FOLLOWING PAGES *An open living and dining room houses an eclectic mix of furniture and art.*

PAGE 152–53 *The stair room and north access corridor feature the first appearance of the newel posts seen in many of Baillie Scott's subsequent houses. The screens connecting the corridor to the stair room were salvaged from an old church.*

Havisham House

Rough Common, Canterbury, Kent, 1911–1912

Magnolia blossoms carpet the entrance courtyard.

RIGHT *The imposing and irregular gabled flint and half-timbered entrance facade convey a Jacobean aura.*

The use of local flint in Havisham House, originally called simply Michael's, reflects the architectural features of the nearby city of Canterbury. The house's site, nestled near the apex of a hill, has a commanding view of the surrounding countryside. The entrance facade is imposing, but Baillie Scott gave it an intimate scale by breaking up the masses in a rambling Jacobean fashion. The front facade of Havisham House has an irregularity which, when combined with the predominance of flint, conjures a deliberately antiquated feel. In fact this facade was initially planted with fast-growing vines to enhance the antique effect. The planting is more restrained now, and when the magnolia tree in the rotunda is in bloom it makes the courtyard with surrounding matured trees an enchanting space.

The garden facade is symmetrical, similar to that at 48
Storey's Way, and its checkerboard motif imitates ancient buildings in Canterbury. The loggias on either end of the house visu-
ally connect the interior and exterior rooms. The gardens are
terraced as a sequence of outdoor "rooms."

The main rooms on the ground floor can all be opened up to
create one contiguous space. The low, beamed ceilings create an
intimacy in a relatively large floor plan. The flow of rooms is
intended to feel unplanned and medieval in character. Of course,
all of the spaces are well thought out and eminently gracious.
The bay windows in the living room and dining room allow copious light as well as an immediate connection to the garden. The
western garden room, with its rounded windows, has now been
recast as the breakfast room, giving the previously dark northern
kitchen access to the southern view.

The carving of the newel posts is of particular interest, being
the most integrated with the stair room and the most intricate
and large carving of any of Baillie Scott's newel posts, with a
variety of flowers and intertwined branches reminiscent of the
stair screen at Blackwell. Kornwolf thought that Havisham
House represented the best example of "craft" in Baillie Scott's
architecture. The detailing and the plasterwork, woodwork,
and brickwork is extraordinary, giving one the impression that
the architect, through his employment of superlative craftsmen, is inviting you to touch and feel each material and surface
in the house.

View through the house from the eastern pergola with all doors open.

RIGHT *A series of terraces leads down to the formal lawn. Jack Snell's ashes are buried under the walnut tree at the end of the rose garden, planted in 1958 when he undertook the initial restoration of Havisham House.*

The plasterwork on the fireplace displays Kentish motifs, the year of completion, and the initials of the original owners.

ABOVE RIGHT A carved beast guards the top of the back staircase.

RIGHT Intricate carving adorns the main-staircase newel posts.

OPPOSITE Corridor accessing all south-facing bedrooms.

The Close

Short Hills, New Jersey, 1912–1913

This unique chapel sits atop the now-enclosed courtyard entrance.

RIGHT *Baillie Scott's only fully half-timbered house belies its New Jersey site.*

The Close is Baillie Scott's only entirely half-timbered house. The architect was absent from the site and the construction was managed by the renowned firm of McKim, Mead & White, who precisely executed Baillie Scott's plans after the client, who wanted a house with the feeling of an old English inn, sent Baillie Scott the outline of his requirements and the architect filled in the details with his usual care.

The chestnut timber for the house was felled from the site and milled into nine-inch-square lumber beams. The house surrounds a charming courtyard, into which the west wing projects at an obtuse angle. The front entrance has been modified to connect the garage and the main house where previously it was possible to drive straight into the courtyard.

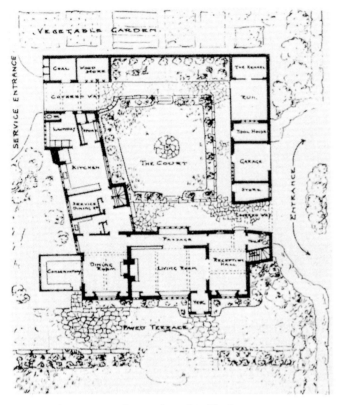

RIGHT *Dining room with original period Stickley furniture.*

FOLLOWING PAGES *More period Stickley furniture, notably the settle, embellishes the living room. Elegant pocket doors open to access not only the corridor but also a bank of window benches.*

The interior planning is similar to that in Baillie Scott's European designs, with window seats, beamed ceilings, and service corridors along the front facade. The house's south wing contains the primary rooms: a hall with staircase, which leads to the living room, the dining room, and a corridor. The west wing contains the kitchen and service areas as well as a stair tower. The north wing contains the front entrance, the garage, a chapel above the entrance on the first level, and a large sleeping porch over the garage, which was originally designed to be completely opened. This large summer lounge-cum-bedroom features removable windows that invite cross breezes.

Baillie Scott's international acclaim preceded him, and the client for The Close, who obviously wanted a genuinely English Arts and Crafts house, was prepared to have Baillie Scott provide the plans from afar. It is ironic that Baillie Scott's most complete half-timbered house is situated in the New World.

Pilgrims

Chilham, Kent, 1912–1921

Deep overhanging eaves and recessed walls enhance the double-height bay windows on the garden facade.

RIGHT *The entrance courtyard with Elizabethan overhanging room on the entrance porch mimics vernacular construction in the nearby village of Chilham.*

Pilgrims is unusual among Baillie Scott's houses because of the duration of the construction process. It was started in 1912 for one of the Sanderson wallpaper heirs, but work stopped at the advent of the First World War, resumed after the war, and was completed in 1921. Pilgrims is similar in many ways to several of Baillie Scott's subsequent houses. A covered carriageway is similar to the entrance at Bill House in Sidmouth and leads into a pleasant courtyard and medieval-style entrance tucked under a cantilevered room. Built of materials similar to the local vernacular, Pilgrims pays homage to the stunning ancient village of nearby Chilham. Pilgrims's setting is ideal, with commanding views of the valley and Chilham church on the neighboring hillside. The garden facade is of particular interest because of Baillie Scott's use of double vertical bay windows, which create recesses with deep eaves.

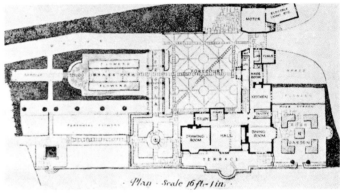

· Plan · Scale 16 ft - 1 in ·

LEFT *The bay window invites the garden in, or the viewer out.*

TOP *Remnants of a past era include the ingenious serving shelf on the kitchen door and the servant's bell next to the fireplace.*

The interior diverges from many of Baillie Scott's previous houses by placing the front entrance on the service wing with a corridor leading to the main south-facing rooms. One of the most interesting survivors from the days of servants is the door connecting the kitchen to the dining room: designed to open normally or to be used as a serving hatch, it is unique to Pilgrims. The low ceiling in the living room is similar to that in Havisham House, though here the living room is brightened by natural light on two sides. The living room acts as a central space with access to the entry hall; the dining room, with a plastered fireplace almost identical to the fireplace in Havisham House; the drawing room, a white space similar to the drawing room in Blackwell; a stair room; and a small study—allowing the owner to monitor the whole house at once. The detailing inside the house is superlative.

171

Gryt-Howe

Cambridge, Cambridgeshire, 1914

LEFT *Exquisite plaster on the diminutive fireplace in the living room.*

RIGHT *The house's strong horizontal profile reflects the flat landscape of Cambridge.*

This small house in Cambridge, built for a bachelor professor of ancient history and his two sisters, has a more utilitarian feel than most of Baillie Scott's houses. Gryt-Howe's proximity to other Baillie Scott houses suggests that academics realized the architect's work represented a new paradigm, and, with limited budgets and a desire to maximize value for their money, they appreciated that Baillie Scott's attention to detail and use of quality materials would stand the test of time. We will never know the exact sequence of events that led to Baillie Scott's following in Cambridge, however, as it is an academic town there would have been considerable social interaction allowing a wider appreciation of Baillie Scott's unique interior planning.

Gryt-Howe's exterior is not remarkable but it does exemplify Baillie Scott's tendency to emphasize the horizontal aspect of his houses through the use of a long steeply pitched roof running the house's entire width and punctuated by a hip-roofed gable. Here the long roofline would fringe the tops of the windows, and the hip-roofed gable would feature hanging tile on its upper half.

Interestingly for a small cottage, the living and dining rooms do not interconnect, indicating the client's request for distinctly separate rooms and not at all in the architect's style. There is wonderful detailing including plasterwork similar to that in Havisham House, and one delightful plastered scene of naked cherubs frolicking. There is one small window vent similar to several windows in Blackwell, a much larger house that, ironically, shares many of the comforts and charms of this, one of Baillie Scott's smaller houses.

Great Wood

Ottershaw, Surrey, 1914

Looking through the great hall window to the garden.

RIGHT *Entrance facade with hanging tiles and herringbone brick between the half-timbering.*

This house, recently split into two dwelling units with considerable sensitivity, represents another striking use of the long sloping roof as a mediating element between modern and traditional architecture. Here the entrance facade gives little indication of what lies within, the great hall that equals any medieval hall, with an imposing fireplace, a minstrels' gallery, a massive beamed ceiling, and a recessed dining room. The hall's function as hub is similar to Undershaw in Guilford.

The house's service area uses pitch pine instead of the ubiquitous oak as a cost-saving measure. As Danish architect Kay Fisker once wrote, "As long as there is still good timber to be had and brick to be fired these materials are just as good and just as 'Modern' as steel and glass."

PRECEDING PAGES
*The separated garden facade
with an added studio alcove.*

LEFT *Baillie Scott
occasionally used pine for
service areas in deference
to his clients' budgets.*

RIGHT *The hall, with
massive fireplace, houses
ingle seats as well as a
dining recess.*

The Tudors

Gerrard's Cross, Buckinghamshire, 1919–1920

LEFT *Similarities to Pilgrims abound in one of Baillie Scott's biggest houses, here deceptively concealed by deep roofs.*

ABOVE *The cavernous lower floor houses the original furnace.*

The Tudors is a particularly fine house where no expense was spared. It is believed that due to Baillie Scott's exacting detail and demands for the highest quality the builder was very nearly bankrupted.

The use of long sloping roofs on the northern side diminishes the scale of the house, and the entry porch with an overhanging room gives this house its Tudor feel. The garage entry is similar to Pilgrims and Bill House. The bricks were handmade and aged. The house was faulted for being deliberately antiquated, with

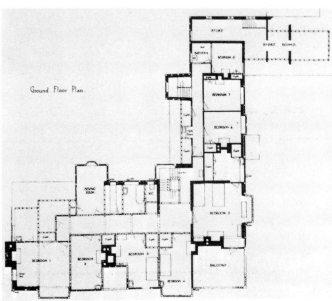

Ground Floor Plan.

TOP *Familiar newel posts and unique oak door latches in the billiards room lead into the great hall.*

RIGHT *The great hall, with library recess and stair room similar to Havisham House and 48 Storey's Way.*

Detail of door latch and bolt on door leading to covered balcony.

OPPOSITE *The upper bedroom corridor, with niche at the end using the motif from 48 Storey's Way.*

FOLLOWING PAGES *View through the exterior window into the second-floor study, which overhangs the entry porch; the lampshade is original.*

critics citing that Tudor artisans would have tried to get lines and levels as true as possible. The imposing three-story garden facade has a wonderful little porch on the first level, which is accessed from one of the extruded double bay windows.

The interior planning is grand but with much less clarity than Baillie Scott's earlier designs. The billiards room alone would suffice as a living room for any large modern house. The main hall has much higher ceilings than is usual in a typical Baillie Scott house, even after the original stone floor was covered by oak floorboards to provide better insulation. The massive oak beams used in the principal rooms could not be sourced or found today. The size of the rooms made careful planning of spaces less critical to the efficient circulation and eliminated the need to create the illusion of space—here there is copious space.

Baillie Scott's mastery of natural light is exemplified in the main hall, with light emanating from the stairwell, the recessed library, the grand bay window, and additional windows on the south wall. One of the unusual features on the interior is the regency dining room. It is a surprise to open the door and find such a refined room, which is in striking contrast to the rest of Baillie Scott's deliberately antiquated design.

Of particular interest is the use of wooden door handles throughout the house, whcih were primarily used in servants' quarters in other Baillie Scott houses. We can only speculate why wooden handles were used so freely here: perhaps to give a rusticated feeling to the house. All have stood the test of time, fully intact and functional. Particularly clever is the use of wooden straps, bolts, and levers for locking doors. The craftsmanship to produce these features is extraordinary, with each piece of hardware the product of years of training. The section of the house that used to contain the servants' quarters has simplified square newel posts and an original sink with its painted oak draining boards intact.

One other particularly fine feature in The Tudors is the airing cupboard with custom-built drawers. Baillie Scott specified only one other such cupboard, for Waldbühl.

The Oak House

Iwerne Minster, Dorset, 1919–1920

The former village hall is nestled in a small lane next to the church.

RIGHT *The long garden facade is accentuated by the ribbon of windows in the original hall.*

Oak House was formerly the Iwerne Minster village hall, commissioned by Sir John Ismay of White Star Line shipping fame. In the days when individuals owned villages, the owner was also the benefactor, and Ismay commissioned the village hall to contain space for a theater, a billiards room, a cards room, and even a shooting gallery in the basement spanning the whole of the length of the hall. On the building's plans there is a "plunge bath" with eight changing stalls.

The exterior planning uses almost identical hipped gables with overhanging rooms to break the mass of the long building on the north and east facades. Baillie Scott used a medley of materials to create the impression of a much older structure that would have evolved over decades of modification and addition.

On Ismay's death the property was reclaimed by his estate and turned into a private residence, much to the dismay of the villagers. It is therefore the most unusual and eclectic of Baillie Scott's residences and does not follow his normal pattern of interior planning. There are five separate sleeping areas, which gives the impression of an authentic Tudor house, as it does not have

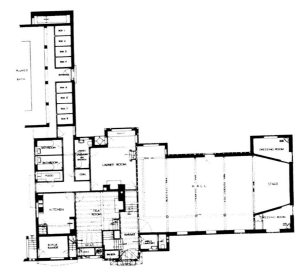

LEFT *Traces of the original stage opening can be seen on either side of the fireplace in the now elegant hall.*

ABOVE *Wonderful artistic license taken by the ironmonger embellishes the handle on the door into the former billiards room.*

a more typically regimented Baillie Scott plan. It is possible to imagine the way the space functioned as a village hall even now.

The great hall at Iwerne Minster is Baillie Scott's greatest, if completely unintentional, residential hall—a magnificent space with ample light provided by the long upper gallery and a bank of windows on the road facade. In an old photograph showing its original use as a hall, two hundred chairs face the stage, which is now walled off to contain the fireplace and, behind that, a bedroom suite. The quality of the craftsmanship is still very much up to Baillie Scott's typically high standards, though the detailing is simpler. The front door is studded with bolts that fit into perfectly crenellated doorposts.

Havelock North

Maidenhead, Berkshire, 1921–1922

Two Ways, now Havelock North, is the second house Baillie Scott built for the Sanderson family and is fabulously situated on the banks of the Thames. The house signaled a new era for Baillie Scott. After the Great War, not only was the economic and social climate vastly altered, so was Baillie Scott's need to maintain a practice while struggling to uphold his ideals and standards, which were increasingly at odds with the progression of postwar modernist architecture.

The house is now separated into two dwelling units, each entirely comfortable. The garden facade contains the great hall, while the front facade faces the river. The tile work on the roof is extraordinary for an English house. The surprisingly shallow hipped gables on the entrance facade emphasize the house's horizontal profile.

The river-facing facade is entirely half-timbered to create the familiar antiquated feel that gives the impression of a structure that appears older than it is. Baillie Scott takes stylistic cues from Pilgrims with the central, double-height bay window, which fits under the roof and creates two interesting recesses with overhanging rooms on opposite sides.

Entrance facade for the north dwelling.

Tiling of a quality rarely seen in England today.

RIGHT *The covered porch leads into the great hall. The eastern facade, with its complex series of bay windows, faces the Thames River.*

Kintail Manor

Saltwood, Kent, 1923

The intimate entrance courtyard has been sensitively redesigned. The front door extrusion is a later addition.

RIGHT *A central column of windows neatly punctures the roof on the garden facade.*

This house, situated on the south coast of Kent, is built in the Kentish tradition with long sloping roofs. The garden facade is particularly interesting because it is evocative of both a traditional Kentish barn and a Tudor manor house. With the dormer window directly above the great hall window Kintail Manor also maintains a very modern profile thanks to this bold column of glass piercing the roof.

The entrance courtyard nestles into the hillside. The front door, though an addition, is well integrated with the overall design. Similarly, the courtyard layout and planting is recent but still sensitive to Baillie Scott's penchant for creating exterior rooms.

The hall is now used as an elegant dining room, the study as the hall, and the dining room has been converted into the kitchen.

OPPOSITE *The stair room with a plethora of newel posts, handy for hauling oneself up to bed.*

FOLLOWING PAGES *Left: The upper corridor accesses a bedroom on either side of the hall and one overhead, reached through the door at the end of the corridor. Right: The view into the hall from the upper corridor.*

Kintail Manor's siting is typical Baillie Scott: it sits on a south-facing hillside and has a sweeping vista that allows views from both the front and rear facades, the former intimate, the latter grand, looking over to Saltwood Castle. The present owner has created the gardens over the last two decades, replacing what was once merely a sloping meadow to the tennis court with intimately landscaped alcoves and well-considered outdoor spaces befitting Baillie Scott and Arts and Crafts garden planning sensibilities.

The interior planning enjoys exceptional clarity for such a late design. The rooms flow as they typically would in Baillie Scott's earlier houses. Also of note is the fact that the original design had only two principle bedrooms and an additional attic bedroom over the great hall, as well as two servants' bedrooms in the east wing. The staircase features classic Baillie Scott newel posts. The two-story great hall has a similar feel to Great Wood and Undershaw, with galleries looking into the space from the corridor and a charming window from the upstairs bedroom tucked high in the corner.

The Gatehouse
Limpsfield Chart, Surrey, 1923

LEFT *The columned bay windows, bell tower, and chimneys balance the symmetrical and horizontal aspect of the garden facade.*

ABOVE *Looking through the entrance facade to the garden, with the billiards room on the left and garage on the right.*

The Gatehouse, situated in Limpsfield Chart near Oxted, Surrey, is built of old Tudor two-inch brick on a flat site, which was originally a level, open field with no trees and, according to Baillie Scott, was the reason for the symmetry on both the front and garden facades. The entrance facade is organized around a courtyard, with two wings housing the billiard room and the garage, while the garden facade has symmetrical corner loggias.

Also on the garden facade is a feature that, by the time of The Gatehouse's design, had become something of a Baillie Scott signature: the double-height bay windows used as columns to break up the facade while serving the purpose of allowing extra light and also deeper eaves on the recesses. The bell tower, though later

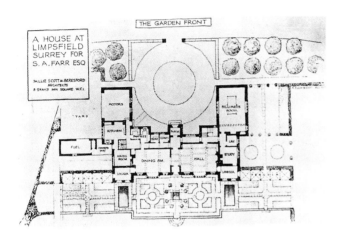

A HOUSE AT
LIMPSFIELD
SURREY FOR
S. A. FARR ESQ

THE GARDEN FRONT

RIGHT *The billiards room with the minstrel's gallery accessed from the staircase.*

FOLLOWING PAGES *Left: View into the living room from the main corridor with open door to the garden and closed double doors leading to the dining room. Right: Main corridor with exposed brick arches.*

added by the client and not on the original architectural plans, is present in the earliest photographs of the house. The garden loggias additionally support the balconies for the primary bedrooms, a feature also seen at Waldbühl.

Baillie Scott uses his usual typical posts in the staircase, which halfway up opens to the minstrels' gallery overlooking the billiards room, featuring in a particularly fine barrel-vaulted ceiling. At the time of construction the use of exposed brick on the downstairs hallways was frowned upon by critics because the use of "outdoor materials" or structural elements on the interior of a Victorian house customarily would have been concealed. Their exposure was a revelation of the Arts and Crafts movement, and, particularly with Baillie Scott, the absolutely honest use of building materials led to a much less formal and more organic form of ornamentation.

Church Rate Corner

Cambridge, Cambridgeshire, 1924

LEFT *Small by Baillie Scott standards, Church Rate Corner is nestled into its private garden amid the bustle of Cambridge.*

ABOVE *What seems to be a closet in the main bedroom leads to a useful changing room.*

Church Rate Corner was Baillie Scott's last commission in Cambridge. This modest house does not have the typical open circulation between living room and dining room. It is, however, packed with Baillie Scott's usual details, exquisite craftsmanship, and efficient use of space.

Orchard House

Crockham Hill, Edenbridge, Kent, 1924–1926

The driveway sweeps down into the entrance courtyard with pronounced entry porch, stair room, and mailbox.

RIGHT Terraces lead down to the garden. The structure at right is a later addition.

Completed in 1926, Orchard House has since had three major additions, but the original core of the house has retained details that reflect local building traditions: long sloping roofs in the Kentish tradition and an entry porch and stair tower that refer to the architecture in the nearby town of Edenbridge. The house is situated on 36 acres and easily has the most spectacular view and grounds of all of Baillie Scott's houses. Situated near the top of a south-facing hill, the house has an unobstructed view of the relatively unpopulated South Downs. The slope of Crockham Hill allows for terracing of the exterior rooms while maintaining the sweeping view.

LEFT *The magnificent grounds offer a sweeping vista of stream, lake, and ancient oaks.*

ABOVE *The thatched folly was originally a milking shed.*

Orchard House is close to Ockhams, where Baillie Scott lived from 1920 to 1942, and Baillie Scott is buried in Edenbridge Churchyard; the current owner of Orchard House has generously restored Edenbridge Church's memorial to Baillie Scott. The property was originally 146 acres, but the original owner donated much of the land to the National Trust, thereby preserving and protecting the surrounding land from development. A walk through the gardens down to a lake surrounded by trees—a scene befitting the grandest of stately homes. A classic 1926 phone box by Sir Gilbert Scott is placed whimsically on the approach to Orchard House, making it feel like a small hamlet. The addition of a postbox in a side wall enhances this impression. The interior follows classic Baillie Scott interior planning, with living room and dining room opening onto each other, northern service corridors, typical detailing, and exquisite craftsmanship. The current owner has replicated the fireplace of Pilgrims in the west study.

Raspit Hill

Ivy Hatch, Sevenoaks, Kent, 1924–1925

The impressive walled entrance courtyard.

RIGHT   *The garden facade has been liberally planted with a variety of evergreens.*

Raspit Hill, one of Baillie Scott's largest houses, has an illustrious past. The house was owned by Thelma Cazalet-Keir, who was Winston Churchill's minister for education. It was also the home of Malcolm MacDonald, the last High Commissioner of Canada and the son of Ramsay MacDonald, and who tragically died at the foot of the stairs in Raspit Hill.

The house is unusual because it was built on the crest of a hill. Even upon first impression, the expansive front courtyard leaves no doubt about the grandeur of the estate. Baillie Scott incorporated many of his best ideas from the previous thirty years into Raspit Hill. The front entry is reminiscent of Havisham House, the covered carriageway of Bill House, the influence of Pilgrims is present on Raspit Hill's east wing, and the sunroom on the

LEFT *The house's enormous scale allows for a cavernous entrance gallery.*

ABOVE *The upper gallery has ample room for a library.*

west end of the house recalls Waldbühl. While the front facade is deliberately imposing, the garden facade, while massive, appears smaller than it actually is due to the height of the roofs and the facade's horizontal profile.

The layout of Raspit Hill is relatively formal, with the scale of the house allowing this more rigid plan. The Regency dining room is reminiscent of that at The Tudors. In addition to a large formal living room there is a morning room for receiving visitors. The north-facing corridors are wide galleries rather than narrow hallways.

At 150 acres, Raspit Hill is the largest estate of Baillie Scott's career, making this and Orchard House, another particularly large estate, unusual. Most of the Baillie Scott houses started as holdings of four or five acres, specifically designed to combine formal gardens, kitchen gardens, and orchards to provide fresh produce year round. Many have fallen victim to the rise in land prices and the desire to speculate on these large properties.

Snowshill Manor

Snowshill, Broadway, Gloustershire, 1926–1927

Charles Wade commissioned Baillie Scott to restore parts of Snowshill Manor and to design the gardens, which are a series of rooms terraced down a hillside with a charming view of the surrounding valley. The manor and grounds now belong to the National Trust and are well maintained by dedicated and knowledgeable groundskeepers.

Features of particular interest in the gardens are the dovecote, the wishing well, a pond with a miniature house, and a working orchard. It is not clear to what extent Baillie Scott was involved in the additions and renovations to the manor—the earliest part of which dates back centuries—as well as the garden design, but it is fair to assume that he would have been one of the premier architects to consult on a project of this scope and scale due to his love of the "old" and desire to have any new structure fit into its environment.

An allée of yew trees leads down to a series of terraced exterior rooms, each with unique features.

The lower terrace features an astronomical clock, a dovecote, and, at left, a well adjacent to the enclosed pond, at right.

Ashwood Place

Woking, Surrey, 1928–1929

The carriage house next to the entrance now contains two four-bedroom apartments.

RIGHT *The imposing garden facade is distinguished by intricate brickwork. Some mystery surrounds the variations in the upper courses on each gable.*

Baillie Scott designed this imposing house for F. J. Derry, who made his fortune by manufacturing women's undergarments fitted with magnets, ostensibly to prevent rheumatism and arthritis. No expense was spared on this, Baillie Scott's largest house. The attention to detail here is astounding, and the architect merged many features from previous houses into the design of Ashwood Place. The similarity to Raspit Hill is obvious, with the imposing front entrance, the wide corridors, and the upper galley. There was originally a morning room, also similar to Raspit Hill's, with fine walnut paneling and ornamental plastered ceilings. The plan and garden facade of Ashwood Place is, in essence, a larger version of The Gatehouse. The design is simple and the proportions are good.

LEFT *An intricately carved screen leads to the garden and into the walnut paneled morning room, below.*

OPPOSITE *A fireplace lined with Delft tiles, impressive andirons, and a grate necessary to heat the imposing main gallery.*

LEFT *The upper gallery is now split into a hall with a Glasgow School sideboard, above, leading to a period dining room, below, with significant Arts and Crafts objects.*

OPPOSITE *Unusually plain newel posts amid stereotypical Baillie Scott detail.*

LEFT AND OPPOSITE *Fireplaces in the original main bedroom suite, left, and dressing room, opposite, are a wonderful fusion of Arts and Crafts, Art Nouveau, and Art Deco.*

BELOW LEFT *The heart carving on the newel post is similar to those found at Waterlow Court and Manderville.*

Ashwood Place had fallen into disrepair by 1996, when it was abandoned after being the National Children's Home headquarters for many years. Michael Wilson, a well-known architect and developer, then embarked on an extensive and sensitive restoration of the house. To give some indication of the remarkable scale of Ashwood Place, the main structure has been converted into seven apartments ranging in size from 1,150 to 1,800 square feet. The high quality of the restoration work makes it almost impossible to see where old and new intersect. Ornamental plaster ceilings have been replicated where originally there were none due to the desire of the architect to give a sense of the original spaces, a rare example of a responsible builder thinking of the well-being of the inhabitants. Much like Baillie Scott, Wilson assembled a team of expert craftsmen who understand quality and exercise it with love and dedication.

The carving in the morning room is especially grand, and the detailing of the laurel leaves on the knees of the Tudor arches is a carryover from Ivydene and many other houses in between. The main bedroom suite has especially fine fireplaces, which combine elements from Arts and Crafts, Art Nouveau, and Art Deco styles.

Witham

Sevenoaks, Kent, 1929

*Simpler than previous houses, Witham still features rich details
in the chimneys, half-timbering, and covered entry porch);
The rear loggia has been enclosed to make a bright study.*

Witham is located in one of three estates in Sevenoaks that were specifically conceived as subdivisions for affluent people who wanted access to the amenities of a country estate in a locale that would be within easy commuting distance of London. Construction on these estates was speculative, and while Baillie Scott railed against mass-produced housing, he resigned himself to the fact that these particular houses were going to be built in any case, so it may as well be his firm that did some of them to ensure that the new owners did have some good design and interior planning.

Witham is a good example of the type of house built on these estates. A relatively modest house, it still functions well and has the advantage of having adjacent land to foster the illusion of space. The layout is similar to Baillie Scott's standard plans, with south-facing main rooms. The architect pays homage once again to local building traditions with hanging tiles and long sloping roofs. The driveway leads through a passageway as was first seen at Bill House and later at Pilgrims and Raspit Hill, though here its form is modest.

Tylers

Sevenoaks, Kent, 1937

Tylers was Baillie Scott's last commission yet still contains elements that were present in his first. The house's exterior reflects the Kentish vernacular with its hanging tiles and long sloping roof. Tylers has a charming service courtyard that has remained essentially untouched for seventy years. Because Baillie Scott's houses are still eminently habitable and their materials are honest and durable, many of the current owners strive to maintain the integrity of the initial design.

The layout is classic Baillie Scott, with a north-facing entry and service corridors upstairs and downstairs. While by 1937 the quality of the craftsmanship was not as fine as his earlier houses, it is still superior for the period. The interior plan for Tylers is remarkably similar to many of Baillie Scott's earlier houses, with the emphasis on good circulation.

Many of those who currently reside in a Baillie Scott house were not familiar with the architect when they moved in, but they almost invariably say they knew instantly that their house was meant for them. It is a great testament to Baillie Scott that the ideas that he first formulated in the late nineteenth century still speak to the people who live in his houses today.

Baillie Scott had the ability to give a strong horizontal aspect to the most imposing houses by banding the brick, hanging tiles, and roof tiles.

Hall and staircase flow effortlessly. The door at right leads to the lavatory conveniently tucked under the stairs, a common Baillie Scott design feature.

OPPOSITE *Front entry porch with carefully arranged mailbox and settle. Solid oak front doors with studs and strap hinges remained a constant throughout the architect's career.*

FOLLOWING PAGES *Left: The view from the kitchen demonstrates Baillie Scott's exemplary interior planning. Though Baillie Scott's latest commission, the house still required a full complement of servants as indicated by the service bells.*
Right: A rare intact service courtyard, with a coal chute door at left, is beautifully embellished.

Acknowledgments

I have two special thanks. The first is for my grandparents, Jack and Claire Snell, who restored, loved, and cared for Havisham House and provided the Snell family with so many treasured memories. And the second is for my parents, Bunty and Sandy Macdonald-Smith, for continuing the care of and sharing the house so generously with family and friends.

The Arts and Crafts movement and I are indebted to Professor James Kornwolf, Diane Haigh, and Greg Slater, who have all fallen under the spell of M. H. Baillie Scott and written books that are academically rigorous and provide a great perspective on the architect, the movement, and his contemporaries.

And more immediately I'd like to thank:

Greg Slater, again, without whom this book would be a shadow of itself, for providing contact information for the Baillie Scott homeowners and for helping to highlight the properties that are exceptional. He also introduced us to his incredible parents, John and Helen Slater, who welcomed us and made our journey to the Isle of Man so special and riotous.

Alexandra Mosher, who patiently waited while I tried to make magic out of the worst summer on record in England. Her styling on the interior shots was invaluable and her creativity a blessing. She helped this project shine, understood that I wanted to see it all, and supported me in achieving the goal of bringing the work of such a great architect to the fore. She is now a reluctant expert on M. H. Baillie Scott!

Peter Kelly of the Victorian Society for his insight and wealth of knowledge of Baillie Scott's Isle of Man era.

John Knaur and Richard Pelkowski of Olympus, Brandon Kirk of Tamrac, Jan Lederman of the MAC Group, and Michael Slater and Edward Sanchez of Nik Software for their generous support.

David Morton, associate publisher at Rizzoli International Publications, for his support, patience, wisdom, and friendship throughout the last fifteen years. This book would be merely a good idea had he not championed Baillie Scott to the publisher, after compiling the definitive work on Frank Lloyd Wright's residential works and being understandably caught out on the significance of Baillie Scott's influence on Wright.

Editor Ron Broadhurst and designer Abigail Sturges above all for their patience in dealing with me when I went to joust windmills for M. H. Baillie Scott on what for most would have been infinitesimal changes, and also for their brilliance in distilling the essence of this giant of the Arts and Crafts movement in such a compact tome.

Last but definitely not least, all the Baillie Scott homeowners who graciously allowed their privacy to be invaded for a few hours. They provided cups of coffee, food, and (occasionally) much-needed showers. This book is really about them because their continued love of their homes allows Baillie Scott's legacy to endure for centuries to come.

An exquisite window vent on a leaded window at the compact Gryt-Howe, a detail first seen at baronial Blackwell.